Through the New Testament

Jeffrey A. Nelson

Augsburg Fortress

Contents

Through the
New Testament
by Jeffrey A. Nelson

Editors: Victor Jortack, Jeffrey S. Nelson,
and Elizabeth Drotning
Cover Designer: Marti Naughton

Scripture quotations are from New Revised Standard
Version Bible, copyright © 1989 Division of Christian
Education of the National Council of the Churches of
Christ in the United States of America. Used by
permission.

ISBN 0-8066-4425-7
Manufactured in U.S.A.
1 2 3 4 5 6 7 8 9 0 1 2 3 4 5 6 7 8 9

Through the New Testament

Through the New Testament is a one-year Bible study course. It recognizes that there are 260 weekdays in a year, and 260 chapters in the New Testament. Each weekday, read one chapter in order through the New Testament, beginning with Matthew 1 all the way through Revelation 22. Weekends are available to "catch up" on any readings missed during the week.

A Bible is needed as the primary text for *Through the New Testament*. The Bible texts themselves are not included. Most translations of the Bible will work well with the included studies even though we have followed the New Revised Standard Version. The design of the studies is to actually train the reader to move deeper into the biblical text, and to learn how to better apply the Bible to daily living.

Record sheets are available for each part of the *Through the New Testament* program. They serve to keep the reader on track for daily reading. When a reading is completed, initial the appropriate space for that chapter. If *Through the New Testament* is being used as a congregational or group program, completed sheets may be turned in for record keeping purposes.

Individual Use

On each weekday, read one chapter from the New Testament. Read these chapters in order, beginning with Matthew 1 and through the end of Revelation. Before you begin each day, take time to ask God to open your heart and mind to reveal God's will for your life through the day's study. It may be of help to read the introduction to the study for the day before actually reading the chapter from the Bible. Only five chapters are to be read each week, one each day. Catch up on any chapters missed during the week on the weekend.

After reading the New Testament chapter, complete the study as part of your reading and reflection. Record your answers, thoughts and questions in the space provided. (You may be surprised after completing *Through the New Testament* to see where you were when you began!) These studies will open the scriptures to you in new ways. The design of the questions in the studies will help you learn how to draw more out of your daily Bible reading. Of greater importance, the studies will allow you to meaningfully apply God's word to your life. Upon completion of your daily study, initial the appropriate space on the record sheet at the back of this workbook. Also, take time at the end of your daily study to say thanks for God's word, and to ask that God might help you to apply your learning to your life.

Couples

Through the New Testament is an excellent way for couples to deepen their relationship and understanding of each other. Set aside time each weekday to do your study together. Pray together aloud before you begin. Take turns reading a paragraph or passage from the Bible chapter for the day. Then use the questions from *Through the New Testament* as a basis for your discussion of the chapter you just read. Record your answers, thoughts, and questions in the spaces provided. Close your time of study with prayer, as well.

Congregational (or Group) Use

Through the New Testament can dramatically increase the biblical literacy of your congregation. There is a greater commitment to participate in and complete the program if it is known that others are also involved. Publicize the program, including the starting date, cost for materials, and any additional offerings to supplement the reading program. Consider a commitment Sunday when those who will participate turn in a commitment card, or are recognized in a significant fashion. (Allow others to join the program later if they wish, but have them begin at the same place as the rest are currently.) We also suggest that each participant be paired with another as "accountability partners" for prayer and to hold another to the commitment.

It is helpful with a congregational reading program to regularly publicize the reading schedule. This insures that all participants are in the same place. Consider printing in the bulletin or newsletter the schedule readings for the coming week or month. As a result of the published schedule, others in the congregation may also do the readings, even though they are not actually part of the program.

Following are some additional ways to keep the program in front of the congregation and to enhance and deepen their learning experience.

Weekly Bible Study

Offer a weekly Bible study on a specific day or evening. The study could be a group discussion or a question-and-answer session led by a pastor or other individual who has some expertise in Bible study. Encourage participants to come with their questions about the readings from the previous week. The leader can answer the questions (It is okay to say, "I don't know."), allow the group to wrestle with the questions, or use them as a springboard for discussion beyond the scope of the studies from *Through the New Testament*.

Preaching Series

Consider preaching each week on a portion of the readings from the previous week. Those participating in the program will welcome a deeper discussion from the pulpit of one of the text they have considered during the week. If you follow a lectionary schedule, let *Through the New Testament* give you permission to choose your own texts for preaching. In fact, *Through the New Testament* provides you the opportunity to address texts that do not normally come up in the course of a lectionary schedule. There may be times during the year when it is necessary to go back to more traditional texts for a particular festival or season. This program, though, can also be a chance to stretch oneself in application of less traditional texts to a particular occasion.

Certificates and/or Awards

The record sheets at the end of *Through the New Testament* allow a pastor in a congregation to monitor the progress of those participating in the program. The pastor may encourage those who have committed to read through the New Testament to turn in each record sheet once it is completed. Keeping track of those who finish the entire one-year reading will make possible to recognize them before the rest of the congregation.

The presentation of a certificate of completion, a Bible lapel pin, or some other award will be greatly appreciated. It may also increase the desire of both those completing and those who did not participate to become involved in this or another program in the future.

Day 1
Matthew 1

Background: Matthew, a Jewish Christian, writes his gospel for Jewish readers. One of his goals is to support his claim that Jesus is the fulfillment of Jewish prophecy. Keep a tally each day of the number of times that Matthew refers to Old Testament prophecies.

(1:1-17) As you read the genealogical record of Jesus, what names do you recognize? Why might Matthew have felt it important to list all these people?

(1:21) "Jesus" is the Greek form of the name "Joshua," which means "the Lord saves." Why is Joseph told to give the baby this name?

(1:20, 24) What is Joseph instructed to do by God? How does Joseph respond? Do you think this was a difficult decision? Explain. What difficult decisions is God asking you to make?

(1:23-25) "Immanuel" and "Emmanuel" mean "God with us." In what ways do you experience God with you in your daily life?

What idea, verse, or phrase from this chapter can change your experience today?

Day 2
Matthew 2

Background: Even though Matthew is a Jew and his readers are Jews, his gospel is not just for Jews. In his writing, Matthew makes it clear that the good news of Jesus Christ is for all people.

(2:1-12) The magi, or wise men, were foreigners who came to worship the newborn king of the Jews. Why might this have been important for Matthew to share with his readers?

(2:16) What does Herod do when he learns that he had missed his chance to kill the newborn king? Why was Herod so anxious to kill this child? When have you heard of someone so concerned with his own situation that he would commit such evil?

This chapter records three different ways that God communicates with people. What are they? How does God speak to you in your life? What things in your life make it difficult for you to hear God's messages to you?

(2:7-23) God takes great care to protect the baby Jesus. How does God work to care for the weak and helpless today? How can you be a part of God's aid to the helpless and needy?

What idea, verse, or phrase from this chapter can change your experience today?

Day 3
Matthew 3

Background: John the baptizer announced his message in a desert region. The food he ate (locusts and honey) was probably the only food available in such an environment. His strange dress (camel hair), food, and lifestyle were a visual protest against self-indulgence. Remember to tally the references that Matthew makes to the Old Testament prophecies!

(3:1-2) John called people to repent. "Repent" literally means "to turn around and go the other way." Are there any things in your life from which you need to turn and go away? If so, what are they?

(3:9) The Jews to whom Matthew was writing were descendants of Abraham, with whom God had a special relationship. John warns against thinking that one's heritage is enough to assure salvation. Might a Christian need the same warning? Explain.

(3:16) In baptism, Jesus identifies with our sinfulness and our need for forgiveness. What meaning does his example have for you?

(3:17) What is one thing you can do today that will make God the Father "well pleased" with you?

What idea, verse, or phrase from this chapter can change your experience today?

Day 4
Matthew 4

Background: Jesus' temptation in the wilderness for 40 days and 40 nights recalls the experiences of Moses (Exodus 24:18; 34:28) and Elijah (1 Kings 19:8), as well as the wandering of the children of Israel for 40 years before God led them into the promised land. The season of Lent is also 40 days long (not counting Sundays). Lent can be a time for us to reflect on our dependence on God as we approach the good news of Christ's resurrection.

(4:1-11) Comment on the fact that Jesus was tempted to sin by the devil before he began his preaching ministry. Do you think this order is significant? Why or why not?

(4:4, 7, 10) Jesus uses scripture to turn back the temptations of Satan. What can you learn from his example?

(4:17) Jesus calls for his followers to repent. "Repent" literally means to turn around and go the other way. What things is Jesus asking you to turn away from and leave behind?

(4:19-22) When did Jesus first call you to follow him? How has Jesus prepared you to respond to his call? Thank him for the difference he has made in your life.

What idea, verse, or phrase from this chapter can change your experience today?

Day 5
Matthew 5

Background: Matthew 5:1-7:29 comprises the most famous block of Jesus' teaching, the Sermon on the Mount. It contains three types of material: (1) declarations of blessedness, (2) encouragement for ethical living, and (3) distinctions between living ethically and just keeping the law.

(5:1-12) This familiar section is called the Beatitudes. Some Bibles begin each beatitude with "blessed," while others use "happy." Happiness here refers to ultimate well-being and spiritual joy. Can you see how these two words might be interchangeable? Explain.

(5:1-12) Those who mourn the way the world is, who hunger for righteous treatment, and so forth will be blessed. What does this suggest for those who work against these things? What of those who fall in between—those who neither mourn and hunger, nor those who work against it? Which group do you fall into?

(5:14-16) Jesus tells us that we can bring light into the dark places of the world. How is God helping you to let your light shine in the darkness? Do you remember to give glory to God when you are praised? Why or why not?

(5:43-48) Who are those whom you have trouble loving? How can Jesus help you to love and pray for them?

What idea, verse, or phrase from this chapter can change your experience today?

Day 6
Matthew 6

Background: This chapter is also part of the Sermon on the Mount. It is not clear to scholars whether Jesus actually taught all these things on one occasion or if Matthew put several teachings together into one large sermon.

(6:1-18) Why does Jesus encourage us to give, pray, and fast in secret? Can you do these things in secret and still give glory to God? Explain.

(6:19-21) What are the three most important things in your life—your treasures? How does this list reflect where your heart is? Are these the kinds of things that can be destroyed by "moth "or "rust"? Explain.

Jesus is always concerned that wealth can get into the way of our relationship with God. In what ways does materialism interfere with your spiritual growth? How do you decide how you will use the wealth God has given you? Do you find joy in your choices in this area? Why or why not?

(6:25-34) This passage is one of the most beautiful and encouraging in Scripture. What is making you anxious today? What does Jesus teach here about your worries? How might you seek God's kingdom more persistently?

What idea, verse, or phrase from this chapter can change your experience today?

Day 7
Matthew 7

Background: Some have dismissed the Sermon on the Mount as being completely unrealistic or as something that will find its fulfillment in the future kingdom. Jesus, though, gave this sermon as a standard for all Christians, realizing that its demands cannot be met by our own power. Instead, we need the power of God to meet these guidelines for living.

(7:1-11) Consider your life in light of these verses. For what have you hesitated asking God? Why have you not asked? How might this passage influence your prayers in the future?

(7:12) This verse is often called the Golden Rule. Has it been difficult for you to keep this guide for living? Why or why not? How might our world be different if everyone followed this rule?

(7:24-27) On what are you building your life? What is your most important goal or priority? Is this thing more like rock or like sand?

(7:29) What things has Jesus said or done in your life that have amazed you?

What idea, verse, or phrase from this chapter can change your experience today?

Background: One of the ways Matthew tries to show that Jesus is the Messiah is through the miracles Jesus performs. That Jesus is God is revealed through his power to heal, to command the forces of nature, and to turn the powers of the devil.

(8:1-13) Consider the relationship between God's great power and our faith. How do these two things work together? What do these two examples of faith teach you about yourself?

(8:5-13) The centurion who comes to ask Jesus for help is a foreigner; in fact, he is the enemy of Jesus' people, the Jews. Why might Matthew have recorded this healing of the servant of an enemy? What does this say about how we should be toward those who are outside our community and whom we might consider "enemies"?

(8:21-22) Jesus may seem insensitive to the disciple who wishes to bury his father. Jesus, though, is saying that commitment to his ministry must come first. What kinds of things is Jesus asking you to leave behind to be a part of his work?

(8:23-34) What storms in your life has Jesus calmed? Take time to thank him for his help. What current turbulence in your life can you ask Jesus to silence now?

What idea, verse, or phrase from this chapter can change your experience today?

Day 9
Matthew 9

Background: Matthew was a tax collector who worked for the Roman government that had occupied Israel. Often these tax collectors cheated the people in order to line their own pockets. A portion of this chapter continues with the theme of discipleship. As you read this chapter, reflect on your own call to be a disciple of Christ.

(9:1-9) Why might Jesus have chosen someone like Matthew to be a disciple? Can you understand why Matthew records the occasions when Jesus spent time with "sinners"? Explain. Do you consider yourself to be among the righteous or among the sinners? What does this teach you about Jesus choosing you to be his disciple?

(9:36) What people do you see today who are "like sheep without a shepherd"? How is Jesus sending you to help the lost sheep? What gifts has God given you to use in this work? How are you using them now?

(9:37-38) Jesus tells us that the "harvest is plentiful." Where are you encountering people who do not know Jesus? Jesus is sending you as a worker to bring in the harvest. Are you working in the right fields—fields that need harvesting? Take time to ask the Lord to send you into his harvest field. Write down the names of three people that you know who do not have a close relationship with the Lord. Say a prayer for each one of them.

What idea, verse, or phrase from this chapter can change your experience today?

Day 10
Matthew 10

Background: This chapter, often called the "sending out of the disciples," is really the commissioning of the twelve apostles for the work they would carry out after Jesus had returned to the Father. His instructions also apply to us who have inherited the Christian commission to go out into the world.

(10:1-42) Consider three specifics to Jesus' instructions. What assignments does he make? What warnings does he give? What comfort does he offer? List them below:

Assignments

Warnings

Comfort

(10:11-16, 40-42) Hospitality is raised up throughout the Bible as an extremely important practice for those who are faithful to God (illustrations of this can be found in Genesis 18:1-19:11, for example). What are some examples of good hospitality being offered by your congregation? What does our congregation do that might cause someone to "shake off the dust from their feet"? What could you do to help welcome the stranger?

(10:17-20) Jesus warns that those who faithfully witness on his behalf may face persecution. When have you suffered persecution for your faith? What might it cost you if you were to fully take up your cross and follow Jesus?

What idea, verse, or phrase from this chapter can change your experience today?

Day 11
Matthew 11

Background: The work of John the baptizer was twofold. First, he tried to call people back to the old covenant relationship they had with God under the Old Testament; second, he pointed the way to the new covenant that people could receive through Jesus Christ. Both positions threatened the power of the leadership of the day, so John was arrested and put into prison. Again, remember to keep track of the references to Old Testament prophecies.

(11:1-6) The Christ for which John and Israel were waiting was to be divine. What evidence does Jesus give that he is indeed the Holy One sent directly from God above?

(11:7-19) In one sense, these words of Jesus might be considered John's funeral sermon. (Matthew 14:1-12 records John's execution.) What does Jesus say that points to John's importance in directing people toward the kingdom of God? What things could be said of your efforts to direct people toward God's kingdom?

(11:25-26) What has Jesus revealed to you? How have these things given new meaning to your life?

(11:28-30) What burden is making you weary in these days? What is the yoke that Jesus offers you? You are free to make this trade today!

What idea, verse, or phrase from this chapter can change your experience today?

Day 12
Matthew 12

Background: The Hebrew word which translates to rested in Genesis 2:3 ("So God blessed the seventh day and hollowed it, because on it God rested from all the work") is the origin for the word Sabbath. In Exodus 20:11, this seventh day of rest is explained as a holy day that should be dedicated to God.

(12:1-14) Jesus tells us here that he is the Lord of the Sabbath. How do the Pharisees react to this statement? How does Jesus' claim affect the man with the shriveled hand? Why might the Pharisees have decided then to kill Jesus?

(12:25-29) The Pharisees accuse Jesus of being Beelzebul, the prince of demons (literally the "lord of flies"). How does Jesus challenge the logic of this claim? When have you seen a house "divided against itself" not stand? What warning does this give to congregations?

(12:30-32) Who are those in today's world that are not with Jesus and thus against him? What are the ways that you are "with Jesus"? In what ways are you working to bring in or stop those who are "against him"?

(12:46-50) What tone of voice do you imagine Jesus using here? What does Jesus mean by these words?

What idea, verse, or phrase from this chapter can change your experience today?

Day 13
Matthew 13

Background: The word parable comes from the Greek word that means "a placing beside." A parable is a story that runs alongside a heavenly truth. When reading a parable, it is helpful to ask certain questions:

Who is God in the story?
Where can I find myself in the story?
How does this lesson speak to my life today?

(13:1-9) Give this parable a title. Answer each of the "parable questions" listed above.

(13:18-23) What kind of ground did the seed of God's Word find in your life? In what ways has that soil changed over the years? Take a few moments to talk to God about the growing conditions in your life.

Title and answer the parable questions for each of these parables:

(13:24-30)

(13:31-32)

(13:44-46)

(13:47-50)

What idea, verse, or phrase from this chapter can change your experience today?

Day 14
Matthew 14

Background: The name Peter, given to Simon by Jesus, comes from the Greek word "petros," which means "rock." Rocks can be solid things on which to build, but they can also be hard and even get in the way of projects. This name for Simon almost becomes a joke in many places. One of those "jokes" is included in this chapter.

(14:1-22) List the things that Jesus did on this particular day. What did Jesus do at the end of this tiring day? What do you usually do at the end of a long, exhausting day? Try ending each day this week following Christ's example.

(14:13-21) Some have tried to explain this miracle by saying that people actually had food with them and simply began to share when they saw the disciples distributing their small amount. Would such an explanation change your view of this as a miracle? How might it open your eyes to other "explainable" miracles that happen in your life?

(14:22-32) At what point does Peter begin to sink (like a rock)? Think back on a time when you took your eyes off of Jesus and began to sink. How did Jesus rescue you? Take a moment to thank Jesus for helping you.

(14:35-36) What does the behavior of the people reveal about their belief in Jesus? What does it say about Jesus' power?

What idea, verse, or phrase from this chapter can change your experience today?

Day 15
Matthew 15

Background: After the Babylonian captivity, the Jewish priests began to make detailed regulations concerning the daily life of the people. These regulations determined what made a person unclean, requiring a sacrifice in the temple to receive God's forgiveness.

(15:8, 18) After the Pharisees challenge Jesus, he turns the tables by challenging them. In these verses, he makes a distinction between the words and actions of people and what is in their hearts. What is in your heart as you think about your relationship with God? Do your actions truly reveal to others how you feel about God? Explain.

(15:21-28) How did you react to the first response of Jesus to the Canaanite woman's request for help? How do you feel about her response to Jesus? What lesson can you learn from this story?

(15:29-31) People were amazed when they saw the results of Jesus' healing on the crowds. What things have you seen God do in people's lives that have amazed you? Has God done anything amazing in your life? Explain.

(15:32-39) When you consider the miracles of Jesus that are recorded in the Scriptures, does it change your thinking about the possibility of the unbelievable happening in your life or church? Why or why not?

What idea, verse, or phrase from this chapter can change your experience today?

Day 16
Matthew 16

Background: We might consider Peter's confession of Christ as the Messiah the very first confirmation. Confirmation (or Affirmation of Baptism) is the public announcement of one's belief in God.

(16:1-12) What do you think Jesus felt when he heard the disciples' words in verse 7? What was Christ trying to tell them? Do you always understand God's messages to you? What can you do today to hear God more clearly?

(16:13-18) What has God revealed to you about Jesus? When was the first time you publicly announced your faith in Christ? When was the last time you told someone about your faith? Try to find an opportunity to tell someone this week!

(16:19) Binding means not forgiving and loosing means forgiving the sins of another. How do you feel about having that kind of power? Does the sacrifice of Jesus on your behalf make it easier for you to loose rather than to bind?

(16:21-28) Have you ever gotten in the way of where Jesus was leading you? Explain. What does the phrase "take up their cross" mean to you? What cross has Jesus given you to carry in his name? In what ways have you had to "deny yourself" to carry this cross? Take a moment to thank God for allowing you to carry a cross as one of God's beloved disciples.

What idea, verse, or phrase from this chapter can change your experience today?

Day 17
Matthew 17

Background: Moses and Elijah are two of the most important figures in Jewish history. Moses represents the old covenant and salvation from slavery. The Jews believe that Elijah will return to announce the coming of the Messiah (thus both John the baptizer and Jesus were said to be Elijah). Indeed, Jesus himself identifies John as Elijah.

(17:1-8) How might Peter and John have felt to be in the presence of not only Jesus, but also of Moses and Elijah? Peter's desire to build dwellings indicates his wish to stay on the mountain with these three. What mountaintop experience have you been reluctant to leave behind? For what ministry did that experience prepare you?

(17:9) Why might Jesus have told his disciples not to reveal to anyone that he was the "Son of Man," a reference to his being God's Son? Why would he want that news kept hidden until after his resurrection?

(17:14-21) What does this event teach you about your faith (especially verses 20-21)? What mountains is God calling you to move? Take a moment to read the prayer in Mark 9:24. Try to make this prayer your own during this week.

(17:26) Jesus' words in this verse imply that his followers belong to God's royal household. What does it mean to you to be a prince or princess in a royal family? Because we have been made members of the royal house, we are free to approach God, our sovereign, and call God "Abba" (roughly translated, "Daddy"). Thank God for this.

What idea, verse, or phrase from this chapter can change your experience today?

Day 18
Matthew 18

Background: Jesus saw the world and the people in it with far different eyes than did others. He was especially mindful of the weak and the helpless. Be mindful of these people as you read this chapter.

(18:1-9) Jesus says that we must become like little children to really receive the kingdom of heaven. What do you think it means to become like a child? How have you done that? What kinds of things prevent you from receiving Jesus like a little child? How can you "cut it off"?

(18:10-14) Who are the lost sheep in our world today? How does Jesus send you to them? Think about the joy you would feel over "one lost sheep" that you helped find. How can those feelings help you to search out those who are lost?

(18:19-20) What do these verses tell you about prayer? What do they say about being part of a community of believers?

(18:21-35) Think about yourself and your life.

For what has God forgiven you?

Have you forgiven people who have hurt or disappointed you?

Are you an unmerciful servant who has been forgiven much but forgives little?

Talk to God about the issue of forgiveness in your life.

What idea, verse, or phrase from this chapter can change your experience today?

Day 19
Matthew 19

Background: It has been said that the purpose of the gospel is to afflict the comfortable and comfort the afflicted. This chapter contains some difficult teachings of Jesus. As you read them, ask yourself, "Do I feel comforted or afflicted?"

(19:1-12) Jesus speaks to the Pharisees and the crowd about looking for loopholes in the commitments they make, in this case with regard to marriage. How do you try to find loopholes to avoid fulfilling your commitments to Jesus? Why do you do this?

(19:14-15) Jesus especially welcomes the least in the kingdom to come to him. When have you felt like one of the least? How has Jesus welcomed you?

(19:16-22) What keeps the young man in this story from having eternal life? What things in life tend to keep you from loving Jesus with all your heart?

(19:23-30) Take a moment to thank God for the wealth you have received. How have you been able to use that wealth to further the kingdom of God? In what ways have you been able to become last so that God may be first in your life?

(19:26) What do you hope for that seems impossible? What dreams do you have for your congregation that seem impossible? Claim the promise of this verse for your life and for your church. How can you work with God to make the impossible possible?

What idea, verse, or phrase from this chapter can change your experience today?

Day 20
Matthew 20

Background: Everything Jesus did was to show us a different set of values for the way we live. The world teaches lessons of materialism and of putting oneself first. What Jesus teaches, on the other hand, frees us from the control of such worldly values. God's ways broaden our view of the world and allow us to share in the work of making the world what God wishes for it to be.

(20:1-16) What qualities of God does this parable reveal? What human characteristics stand in contrast to the nature of God?

(20:20-28) What similarities do you see between this event and the parable Jesus told in 20:1-16? Does it surprise you that any of the disciples could make such a request? Explain. How does their lack of understanding of Jesus' teachings help you when you have difficulty with his words to you?

(20:26-28) These verses point out another contrast between God's values and human values.

How did Christ serve?

How can you serve someone today?

(20:29-34) Have you ever asked Jesus for mercy? What might that mean? How would you answer if Jesus asked you, "What do you want me to do for you?"

What idea, verse, or phrase from this chapter can change your experience today?

Day 21
Matthew 21

Background: Jesus' entry into Jerusalem helped to fulfill the prophecies of the Old Testament about the coming of the Savior. Keep in mind that these prophecies were given to people by God long before Jesus was born. It would have been extremely difficult, if not impossible, for someone to coordinate such an event to present himself as the Savior. Only the true Christ could have done this.

(21:1-11) Imagine that you were on the streets of Jerusalem when Jesus rode in as the king. What would you have laid at his feet? What are you willing to lay at his feet today to show that you acknowledge him as your king?

(21:12) What does this incident tell you about the human characteristics of Jesus? Consider his physical build and his emotions in your response.

(21:12-17) If Jesus visited your congregation, can you think of anything that might make him angry? What would he see that would make him happy?

(21:18-22) Jesus' cursing of the fig tree is a reminder to all of us of the importance of bearing fruit for Christ. What fruit are you bearing for Jesus today? How can you claim the promise of verse 21 for yourself?

(21:33-46) In the parable of the tenants, who are the tenants? The servants? The son? Why did the religious leaders so fear Jesus and his teachings?

What idea, verse, or phrase from this chapter can change your experience today?

Day 22
Matthew 22

Background: Jesus' teachings become more urgent as he drew nearer to his death. While reading this chapter, consider the things Jesus says in light of his impending crucifixion and the end of his earthly ministry.

(22:1-14) Who invited you to be a part of God's great banquet? As one of God's servants, whom are you inviting to come to the banquet? Remember that not everyone who is invited will come. Still our sovereign encourages us to continue to faithfully invite.

(22:15-22) What has God given to you? Have you been faithful in your stewardship of what God has given you? Make a specific commitment today of what you will give back to God.

(22:23-40) Who will you look forward to seeing at the resurrection of the dead? What does it mean to you that everyone will be "like angels"?

(22:34-40) What is the motive of the Pharisees as they ask this question? What lesson does Jesus teach in his response? How are you keeping this greatest commandment?

(22:41-46) Jesus' response is meant to show that the Savior (Son of Man) was more than the son of David—he was David's Lord. In what ways do you declare Jesus to be your Lord?

What idea, verse, or phrase from this chapter can change your experience today?

Day 23
Matthew 23

Background: This chapter comprises a sharply worded discourse by Jesus, criticizing the religious practices and lifestyle of the Pharisees and Sadducees, the religious leaders of Jesus' day. These words serve as a caution to all of us not to use religion as a basis for judging others or for lording one's position over others.

(23:1-12) What is Jesus warning against in this section? Who are those in our world today who seek titles in prideful fashion? When have you become great by being the servant of others?

(23:13-32) This section contains seven "woes". What does each woe warn against?

(23:13-14)

(23:15)

(23:16-22)

(23:23-24)

(23:25-26)

(23:27-28)

(23:29-32)

What overall theme would you give to this entire chapter? What needs to be cleansed from your heart?

What idea, verse, or phrase from this chapter can change your experience today?

Day 24
Matthew 24

Background: Before Jesus leaves his followers, he cautions them and gives them signs that will indicate his return. Throughout history, there have been those who have predicted the return of Christ. Keep this in mind as you read Jesus' words.

(24:9-14) The persecutions that Christians suffered in the first century after Jesus' death and resurrection were much more severe than those faced by most of us today. Have you ever been persecuted or suffered for your faith? Explain. What other religious persecution do you see in the world today?

(24:23-28) Who are the false messiahs and false prophets in the world today? What messages are leading people away from the one true Christ? How can you help them to hear the voice of the Savior?

(24:36-44) Why doesn't Jesus give us more specific details about when he will return? If you knew Christ would come back this Saturday, how would you live differently between now and then?

(24:45-51) Of what important things has the master put you in charge? Have you been a faithful and wise servant? What do you hope the master will find you doing when he returns?

What idea, verse, or phrase from this chapter can change your experience today?

Day 25
Matthew 25

Background: The term talent was first used for a unit of weight—approximately 75 pounds. Later it was used for a unit of coin. A talent was equal to 60 minas; a mina equaled 100 drachmas. A drachma was worth one day's wages. Our present day use of "talent" as an ability or a gift comes from the parable of the talents in this chapter.

(25:1-13) What is the distinction between the wise virgins and the foolish virgins? What does the oil represent in this parable? How are you making sure that you have enough "oil" to last until the return of Christ?

(25:14-30) With what things have you been entrusted? To what degree are you using them? For what purpose?

(25:29) Have you ever been given "more" in recognition of what you accomplished? Explain. What have you done with this?

(25:31-46) Look around you. Do you see hungry, thirsty, naked, sick, or imprisoned people? Who are they? Make a firm resolution to meet the needs of someone this week. In this way you will be ministering both for and to Christ.

What idea, verse, or phrase from this chapter can change your experience today?

Day 26
Matthew 26

Background: Throughout Jesus' life, he tried to teach others a new way of living in relationship to God. The Passover meal that we remember as the Lord's Supper is perhaps the greatest example of this. Jesus takes the greatest festival of the Jewish faith and through it and his death gives us a new and personal way of relating to our heavenly Father.

(26:1-16) What contrasts do you see between the woman at Bethany and Judas Iscariot? What do they do and why? How do you show your love for Jesus? How do you betray him?

(26:31-35, 69-75) When have you, like Peter, made vows of loyalty to Jesus and then broken them by your words or actions? How did you deal with your stumbling?

(26:36-44) Jesus prayed often. In this case, prayer helped to sustain him through an extremely trying situation. How has prayer supported you through trials in life? Have you ever felt the special encouragement of knowing that others have joined you in prayer (encouragement Jesus did not enjoy in this case)? Explain.

(26:47-56) Why does Jesus allow himself to be arrested in this fashion? What does this tell you about Jesus?

What idea, verse, or phrase from this chapter can change your experience today?

Day 27
Matthew 27

Background: The occupying Romans had forbidden the Jews to carry out an execution. Thus, it was necessary for them to bring Jesus before Pontius Pilate, the Roman governor of that region. Only Pilate could give the command to have someone put to death.

(27:1-10) What is it that leads Judas to return his reward and to kill himself? Why do you think one who lived so long with Jesus could have so misunderstood who he was?

(27:11-26) How could the crowd that had just a few days before received Jesus as king now call for his death? What happens when leaders blindly lead a crowd? How can you avoid being misled?

(27:46) Was Jesus really abandoned by God? Explain. When have you felt that God had forsaken you? How were you reassured of God's presence in your life?

(27:50-54) What signs show that God is still at work in the crucifixion? What do you think is the significance of the torn temple curtain in verse 51?

(27:62-66) What do the chief priests and Pharisees mean by "the last deception" and "the first"? About what are they concerned?

What idea, verse, or phrase from this chapter can change your experience today?

Day 28
Matthew 28

Background: Matthew is the only gospel writer who records the posting of the guard at the tomb (27:62-66). In this chapter he also gives the report of the guards following Jesus' resurrection. Remember that Matthew writes his gospel for a Jewish audience who has heard the reports that were circulated by the soldiers.

(28:1-10) What emotions are present in the various individuals mentioned in this passage? Are you surprised by the mixture of feelings experienced by the women in verse 8? Explain. What emotions do you experience as you read this chapter?

(28:11-15) Why are the chief priests so desperate to stop the report of the Roman soldiers? What does the failure of their plan tell you?

(28:16-17) What events have inspired you to worship Jesus? What has caused you to doubt? How have you overcome your doubts and continued to worship him?

(28:19-20a) What is Jesus' last command to his people? The word "go" could be also translated "while you are going." What does that imply to you as you seek to fulfill this command?

(28:20b) What promise accompanies Jesus' command? What does that mean for you? When have you claimed that promise?

What idea, verse, or phrase from this chapter can change your experience today?

Day 29
Mark 1

Background: The writer of this gospel is generally thought to be John Mark of the Book of Acts (Acts 12:12, 25). Mark's gospel may actually be a record of the preaching and teaching of the disciple Simon Peter, recorded by Mark. This is considered the earliest written gospel of the New Testament. Keep count of how often Mark uses the words and phrases *as soon as, at once, at this,* and *immediately* in his writing.

Mark does not begin his gospel with the birth of Jesus. Why might that be? Is the story of the birth of Jesus important to you? Why or why not?

(1:1) The word gospel literally translates as "good news"; the name "Jesus" means "God saves"; and the title "Christ" means "anointed one." (Anointing was a sign of having been set apart to serve God.) What is the good news that Mark wants to tell his readers? How has it been good news in your life?

(1:16-20) In what areas of your life is Jesus saying, "Follow me"? What, if anything, must you leave behind to truly answer his call?

(1:35) Notice that Jesus takes time to pray between healing and teaching. What does this teach you about dealing with the busyness of your life? When do you take time to go off to a solitary place to be with God?

What idea, verse, or phrase from this chapter can change your experience today?

Day 30
Mark 2

Background: For Jews, the Sabbath begins on Friday evening at sundown and ends Saturday at sundown. This is the holy day to rest and spend time worshiping God. Many Christians worship on Sunday because it is the day on which Jesus rose from the dead—each Sunday is a "little Easter."

(2:1-5) Whose faith is it that Jesus takes note of in this healing narrative? What does this say to you about the importance of a Christian community? Have you ever worked to help bring healing to a friend? When?

(2:5-12) Why do you think Jesus forgave the man's sins before healing his illness? What does the healing say about Jesus' power? Which do you need more from Jesus—forgiveness or healing? Explain.

(2:13-17) Who is it that Jesus has come to save? Why do the Pharisees not see themselves in need of Jesus' healing? Who are you more like in this story? Why?

(2:23-28) Does it make sense that religious laws could be more important than the needs of people? Why or why not? In what ways have religious traditions and requirements gotten in the way of worshiping and serving God? How might we change these things?

What idea, verse, or phrase from this chapter can change your experience today?

Day 31
Mark 3

Background: Jesus was rejected by the Jews who were in authority in those days—the Pharisees, Herodians (supporters of Rome), Sadducees, and others. These people represented the twelve tribes of Israel. Jesus' selection of twelve disciples was symbolic of creating a new Israel to replace the old Israel that refused to receive him as the Messiah.

(3:1-6) Why might some people have wanted to trap or accuse Jesus? How does Jesus' question in verse 4 turn the tables on them? What does this passage suggest to you for the ministry of your congregation and your own personal ministry?

(3:7-12) The areas mentioned in this passage comprise most of Israel as well as many surrounding areas. Why would Jesus attract people from so many areas? What first attracted you to Jesus? How far (not just geographically) have you traveled to be with Jesus?

(3:13-15) Jesus was intentional about choosing and training people based on their gifts. What gifts has God given you? (If you're not sure, talk to a pastor about completing a spiritual gifts inventory.) How is God calling and training you to use your gifts?

(3:20-35) What are the various ways that the people in this chapter see Jesus? Why does the view of the teachers of the law (Pharisees and Sadducees) not make sense? How do you think of Jesus?

What idea, verse, or phrase from this chapter can change your experience today?

Day 32
Mark 4

Background: A parable usually is set in a situation that is familiar to most people. Its purpose is to reveal a spiritual or moral truth. As you read these parables, consider how the truth contained is both hidden and revealed.

(4:1-8) The parable of the sower. What can you do to make your life "good soil" for God's word?

(4:21-23) A lamp under a bushel basket. What have you done recently to let your light shine for Jesus?

(4:26-29) The parable of the growing seed. In the parable of the sower, we are the soil to receive the word of God. Who are we in this parable?

(4:30-32) The parable of the mustard seed. Jesus' ministry with twelve followers began as something quite small and insignificant. What great things is it producing today?

(4:24-25) As you read God's word each day, are these verses a message you welcome or fear? Explain.

(4:35-41) Mark makes it very clear that Jesus is Lord, not only over his church but also over all of creation. Are you surprised by the response of the disciples to Jesus' miracle? Explain. How would you answer their question in the last verse?

What idea, verse, or phrase from this chapter can change your experience today?

Day 33
Mark 5

Background: Mark uses words like immediately more than 40 times in his gospel. Mark feels great immediacy about conveying the good news of Jesus to his readers.

What qualities or characteristics of Jesus do you find in these narratives of some of his miracles? Do these qualities fit your image of Jesus? Explain.

The miracles of Jesus show his power with forces over which we seem powerless. List that over which Jesus is Lord in each passage:

(5:1-13)

(5:25-34)

(5:21-24, 35-43)

(5:34, 36) What do Jesus' words in each of these verses suggest to you? When have you trusted Jesus with physical needs? What led you to put your faith in him? What healing did you receive from him?

(5:18-19) Do Jesus' words to this man surprise you? Why or why not? To what friend or family member is Jesus telling you to go? What things has the Lord done for you that you will tell this person?

What idea, verse, or phrase from this chapter can change your experience today?

Day 34
Mark 6

Background: Mark's gospel is written primarily to the Romans, the most powerful empire in the world at that time. To impress the Romans with the power of Jesus (even greater than their own), Mark focuses on the miracles and authoritative teachings of Jesus.

What qualities or characteristics of Jesus do you find in these narratives of some of his miraculous works? Would these impress the citizens of the great Roman Empire? Explain. What do they say to you?

(6:1-6) The question about Jesus being a carpenter (verse 3) implies that a common worker could not have anything significant to say on his own. Do you agree or disagree? Have you known any "common workers" who had faith-building gifts to share?

(6:7) For what reasons would Jesus have sent the disciples out in pairs? When have you seen this put into practice?

(6:8-11) Why might the disciples have been told to take nothing? What lesson is here for congregations? What warning?

(6:30-56) What can you contribute to help meet the needs of others? What needs do you have that you would like Jesus to satisfy? Take a few moments to bring these before him right now.

What idea, verse, or phrase from this chapter can change your experience today?

Day 35
Mark 7

Background: Mark on several occasions records the Aramaic words spoken by Jesus (like Corban in 7:11 and Ephphatha in 7:34). Because he is writing to a Roman audience, though, Mark takes time to translate these words for his readers who would be unfamiliar with the terms.

(7:1-13) The Pharisees, Jewish religious teachers, stressed the keeping of not only the scriptural laws but also the religious traditions of the day. What traditions in churches today have practically become laws? How do these stand in the way of accomplishing Jesus' will?

(7:14-23) Are there any "unclean" things that you are saying or doing from which you would like to be free? How are these things separating you from God? Ask God to help you shed these unclean practices.

(7:24-30) This passage marks a change as Jesus now brings his message and ministry to non-Jews. What does the woman's answer reveal about her? How does Jesus respond to her answer? Are you amazed by Jesus' power?

(7:31-37) Note how many people are aware of Jesus and come to him for help. Besides the miracles he performs, what more might these people, oppressed by the Romans, want from Jesus? Can you explain why Jesus would ask the healed man to keep silent about his healing?

What idea, verse, or phrase from this chapter can change your experience today?

Day 36
Mark 8

Background: One of the most important themes in Mark's gospel is that of discipleship. Jesus' teachings about discipleship often follow his predictions of his death. Discipleship is demonstrated most clearly in the ultimate sacrifice made for another.

(8:1-10) Are your responses to God's call to serve ever like the disciples' (verse 4)? Explain. What amazing things might Jesus do with your help?

(8:11-13) The Pharisees ask for a sign from heaven. How has God revealed God's self in your life this week?

(8:27-30) How do you answer the question Jesus asked Peter: "But who do you say that I am?" Jesus told his disciples not to tell anyone. What does Jesus tell you to do with this knowledge (see Matthew 28:18-20)? How well are you doing with this great commission?

(8:34-37) Discipleship—following Christ as a disciple—means putting Christ's mission first. What is Christ asking from you as a disciple? How difficult or easy has it been for you?

What idea, verse, or phrase from this chapter can change your experience today?

Day 37
Mark 9

Background: In the New Testament, sickness is understood to come from the devil. Often those who were brought to Jesus for healing were either possessed by or were ill because of evil spirits (demons). The reaction of these evil spirits to Jesus shows that he is Lord of all creation.

(9:2-10) A voice from above tells Jesus' disciples to listen to him. What is he saying to you? Are you listening to Jesus? Explain.

(9:24) The father of this possessed boy passionately expresses his faith, but also his doubts. Have you ever been moved to cry out in faith and/or doubt? If so, when? How has God helped you to over-come your unbelief?

(9:33-35) Why is it so difficult to consider being last instead of trying to be first? How did Jesus become servant of all? How might you be a servant to someone today?

(9:38-49) When have you seen one group of Christians trying to stop another because they were not a part of their group? How does this deny the work of the Holy Spirit? How can we be more open to the ministry of other groups?

What idea, verse, or phrase from this chapter can change your experience today?

Day 38
Mark 10

Background: In all his teachings, Jesus shows his concern that nothing get in the way of a person's growth in relationship to God. Religious rules, adult beliefs, material possessions, and personal desires are just some of the things that can interfere with what should be most important: our connection to God.

(10:9) Jesus says here that God is present in the marriage relationship. How might the relationships between husbands and wives change if they strove to keep God active in their marriages? In what relationships in your life do you sense God's presence?

(10:13-16) How are children today kept from coming close to and being blessed by Jesus? What can you do to change this? Take a moment to ask for God's help in this.

(10:17-31) Jesus is not saying that wealth is sinful. Rather, it is what we do with our wealth that may or may not be sinful. In what ways does your wealth get in the way of your relationship with God? In what ways are you using your wealth to give glory to God?

(10:42-45) In verse 45, what does Jesus say is the reason for giving his life? How does this make you feel? Thank Jesus for paying the price for your release.

What idea, verse, or phrase from this chapter can change your experience today?

Day 39
Mark 11

Background: An important theme in Mark's gospel is that Jesus' death was his own will, that he was not helpless to the powerful Romans. Pay attention to this as you read the next few chapters that record the final week of Jesus' life before the crucifixion.

(11:10) For what kind of kingdom were the people in Jerusalem looking? How would the religious and political leaders of Jesus' day have felt about this? What kind of kingdom was Jesus offering?

(11:12-14, 20-21) The New Testament teaches that Satan is responsible for hunger. How might this explain Jesus' action toward the barren tree?

(11:15-19) Pilgrims coming from great distances would need to change their foreign currency and purchase animals for temple sacrifice. The moneychangers and sellers charged unfairly high fees although these pilgrims would have no choice but to pay. Why does this anger Jesus? What might Jesus want to overturn in your life to cleanse you? Will you let him?

(11:22-24) What great mountain is God challenging you or our congregation to move? Do you have faith enough that it can happen? Have you prayed that this might happen? Take a moment to do so now.

What idea, verse, or phrase from this chapter can change your experience today?

Day 40
Mark 12

Background: Many of Jesus' actions and words in this chapter are designed to force opponents to take action against him. They also illustrate the urgency Jesus now feels in his last days to teach his followers lessons that are necessary for their life without him.

(12:1-12) In this parable, the owner of the vineyard is God and the servants first sent are the Old Testament prophets. Who is the son and who are the tenants? Why does this story cause the religious leaders to seek to have Jesus arrested?

(12:13-17) How was this a trap for Jesus? What responsibilities do we have to our government that do not infringe upon our responsibilities to God? (You may want to read Romans 13:1-7.) What governmental rules, if any, is God calling you to challenge?

(12:28-34) Write down the two parts of the Great Commandment. How does this commandment encompass all of the Ten Commandments (Deuteronomy 5:7-21)? Which part of the Great Commandment is easier for you to follow? Why?

(12:41-44) Why does Jesus find the widow's small offering worthy of praise? Why might such a poor woman give anything? Are you giving out of your poverty or out of your wealth? Explain?

What idea, verse, or phrase from this chapter can change your experience today?

Day 41
Mark 13

Background: This discourse falls into five sections: (1) prediction of the destruction of the temple in Jerusalem (which did occur in the year 70 A.D.) and the question of the disciples, (2) warnings against deceivers and false signs of the end, (3) the return of Christ, (4) the lesson of the fig tree, and (5) a call to watchfulness.

(13:5-23) What things do you hear in today's world that seems to suggest that Christ will soon return? For what things does Jesus say to watch out (verses 5, 9, 23, 33, 35, 37)? Can you think of any examples of these kinds of things?

(13:12-13) Have you seen families divided over faith in Jesus? How do you think God feels about it? How can you help believers to stand firm in their faith? Can you think of anyone who needs this kind of support now?

(13:32-37) What does Jesus say that can help you to continue calmly on your course of faith when signs of the end times appear? If you knew Jesus was going to return tomorrow, what would you like him to find you doing? Why? Is it different from what you would normally be doing? Why or why not? What changes might you make in your life so that each day you might be found doing that which is pleasing to God?

What idea, verse, or phrase from this chapter can change your experience today?

Day 42
Mark 14

Background: Scholars believe that the Lord's Last Supper may have been eaten at the home of John Mark's parents. Mark would have been just a teenager or young man at the time; perhaps he even waited on Jesus and the disciples during the meal. Having witnessed those events, he may have followed them to the garden where he saw Jesus arrested and was the young man in the linen cloth (verse 51).

(14:1-9) How do you think this woman felt about Jesus? If you could, what would you do to show your feelings for Jesus?

(14:17-26) The Last Supper was the celebration of the Passover commemorating the time when the angel of the Lord passed over the homes of the Hebrews rather than killing their firstborn sons, as the angel did in the Egyptian homes (see Exodus 12:1-14). How does Jesus change this meal to create a new relationship between God and Jesus' disciples? When you receive the Lord's Supper in worship, what emotions do you experience? Why?

(14:32-72) When have you had to wrestle between your will and God's will? Which did you choose? How did that experience affect your relationship with God? What did you learn about God? What did you learn about yourself?

What idea, verse, or phrase from this chapter can change your experience today?

Day 43
Mark 15

Background: Recall that Mark's gospel is targeted to the Romans. This makes the statement of the Roman centurion (in charge of 100 soldiers) in verse 39 very significant. His pronouncement also completes what Mark stated in 1:1 of his gospel.

(15:1-5) Reflect on how Jesus presents himself before Pilate (and the Sanhedrin in 14:53-65). What do you admire about Jesus in these situations? What surprises you about his behavior?

(15:21) Simon of Cyrene (in northern Africa) likely was a Jew visiting Jerusalem to celebrate the Passover. His sons, Alexander and Rufus (see Romans 16:13), apparently were well known to those to whom Mark wrote. With their parents, they became followers of Jesus. With whom have you most sought to share your faith so that they might know Jesus? Where are they in their faith journey now? How does this make you feel?

(15:39) What do you think moved the centurion to make this confession of faith? What finally led you to confess Jesus as your Lord? How has your confession changed your life? Take a moment to thank God for your faith.

(15:42-47) Joseph of Arimathea acted at great risk to himself and his position in the community. What risks have you taken to serve Jesus?

What idea, verse, or phrase from this chapter can change your experience today?

Day 44
Mark 16

Background: The most reliable early manuscripts do not include Mark 16:9-20. It is believed that the actual end of Mark's gospel was lost and that the early Church added this final portion. We should not, however, allow this to diminish the value of Mark's gospel to us.

(16:1-8) The bringing of spices was an act of devotion and love toward Jesus, even in death. In what ways do you like to show your love and devotion to Jesus? In what ways have you been surprised as you have come to Jesus?

(16:9-13) Why do you think it is so difficult for some people to believe the good news that Jesus has to offer? When have you struggled to believe the amazing story of God's love through Jesus? What helped you through your struggle?

(16:14-18) How does Jesus scold the disciples? How does he encourage them? What assignment does Jesus give to his followers? How will you preach the good news in the world today? What is the most important thing you want others to know about Jesus?

(16:20) In what ways will you trust that Jesus will work with you as you share the good news? How can that trust send you into places or encourage you to say things that you wouldn't otherwise? Ask Jesus to go with you today.

What idea, verse, or phrase from this chapter can change your experience today?

Day 45
Luke 1

Background: Luke is a physician (see Colossians 4:14). As a doctor, Luke pays attention to the medical aspects of certain narratives. For example, only two types of people would note the kicking of an unborn baby in his mother's womb (Luke 1:41)—a mother or a doctor. Take note of the special medical insights that Dr. Luke offers in his gospel.

(1:1-4) To whom is this "orderly account" written? Theophilus means "one who loves God." How do others know that you love God?

(1:5-25) Does Zechariah's response to the angel Gabriel surprises you? Explain. Does God's response to Zechariah's question seem harsh? What might Zechariah have thought about in silence during Elizabeth's pregnancy?

(1:26-38) In Luke's day there were those who taught that Jesus was not really God, but was adopted by God at his baptism. How would this passage support the idea that Jesus is God? What does Mary's response to Gabriel tell you about her? Has God ever set a task in front of you? How did you respond?

(1:46-55) This passage is called Mary's song of praise or the Magnificat. What emotions does Mary reveal in her song? For what do you praise God?

What idea, verse, or phrase from this chapter can change your experience today?

Day 46
Luke 2

Background: Some scholars believe that Luke may have interviewed Mary about the life of her son. In fact, only Mary could have told some of the narratives in this gospel. Perhaps this is really the Gospel of Mary, as written by Dr. Luke.

(2:1-3) Luke's gospel reveals him to be not only a doctor, but also a historian. Look at Micah 5:2. Does it amaze you that God can use the decree of a Roman emperor to fulfill this prophecy? Explain.

(2:8-20) What are the three different responses of the shepherds to the message of the angels? When have you experienced any of these responses to the good news of Jesus Christ?

(2:21) Circumcision was a very important rite of passage to the Jews as they sought to be faithful to God. In what religious rites have you participated? Of what importance was each rite to you?

(2:25-35) How did Simeon know who this baby was? What has the Holy Spirit revealed to you about Jesus? Thank the Holy Spirit for this gift.

(2:41-50) If you had been Jesus' parent, how would you have reacted to this event? Might your response be different if angels had foretold the birth of your child? How would you feel about your child putting our heavenly Father above all else?

What idea, verse, or phrase from this chapter can change your experience today?

Day 47
Luke 3

Background: Matthew's genealogy of Jesus (1:2-16) follows the line of Joseph (Jesus' legal father). This would have been important to the Jewish people to whom he was writing. Luke's genealogy traces the line of Mary (Jesus' blood relative). Luke probably does this to again affirm the virgin birth of Jesus from chapters 1 and 2.

(3:1-6) How does John fulfill the prophecy of Isaiah 40:3-5? Why might Luke have felt this was important to record? Before a king journeyed to a distant country, the roads he would travel were improved. In your life, what valleys must be filled and mountains leveled to prepare for the coming of Jesus?

(3:7-14) What does John tell his listeners that they should do? Why does he tell them to should do these things?

(3:15-18) Why does Luke call this message of John "good news" or "gospel"? How has it been good news to you? Notice how John humbles himself as he points to the true Messiah or Christ. When have you given the glory to Jesus instead of taking it for yourself? How did you feel when you did that?

(3:23-37) What names do you recognize from the list of Jesus' ancestors? Why do you think Luke follows this family tree through the entire human race? Have you ever considered that one of your ancestors is God?

What idea, verse, or phrase from this chapter can change your experience today?

Day 48
Luke 4

Background: More than any other gospel writer, Luke emphasizes the work of the Holy Spirit. As you read Luke's Gospel, pay attention to the presence of the Holy Spirit. Consider how the Holy Spirit has been involved in your life.

(4:1-13) Give a one-word description to each of the three temptations of Jesus. Has the devil ever used one of these temptations against you? Explain. What does this passage teach you about the importance of knowing Scripture? What comfort do you get from knowing that Jesus, like us, experienced temptation?

(4:14-21) What does this passage tell you about Jesus' worship practices? Why do you think this was important for Jesus? Why is it important for you? How does Jesus show he was anointed? Has God anointed you? Explain.

(4:22-30) Why was the crowd so angry with Jesus? Why would a mob choose to take such extreme action? How does Jesus handle this situation? What does that suggest to you about Jesus?

(4:38-44) What does this passage tell you about Jesus' concern for the people? What does Jesus say is the main focus for his ministry? If you could choose between Jesus' healing and preaching, which would you choose? Why?

What idea, verse, or phrase from this chapter can change your experience today?

Day 49
Luke 5

Background: Matthew, Mark, and Luke are called synoptic gospels because they use much of the same stories and language. (The word synoptic literally means "seen as one.") Most scholars believe that both Matthew and Luke used Mark's Gospel as the core of each of their gospels. Each of the two later gospels added information to support the message they wanted to present to their readers.

(5:1-11) By setting out in the boat, Jesus uses the water of the lake as a natural amplifier so that more people could hear his teachings. What would have caused Simon to be so responsive to Jesus' request? How do you explain the large catch of fish? How do you explain Simon Peter and his partners so quickly leaving their business to follow Jesus?

(5:12-13) Leprosy was an easily spread skin disease that was often fatal. Why would Jesus' touch be so important to this man? What inner healing do you think this man received?

(4:42, 5:16, 6:12) What pattern is revealed in these verses? Do you follow Jesus' example in this case? Why or why not?

(5:27-39) Levi (Matthew) throws a great banquet when he is accepted and called by Jesus. Who does he invite? Why would he invite these people? Who would you invite? Why don't you? After all, Jesus has called you, too!

What idea, verse, or phrase from this chapter can change your experience today?

Day 50
Luke 6

Background: A distinction is made between disciples and apostles. Disciples were those who regularly followed Jesus and were committed to his teachings. Apostles (meaning "ones sent with a special commission") were disciples who were given the special responsibility of sharing the message of Jesus.

(6:12-16) What does Jesus do before he selected the twelve who would be his apostles? Before what important tasks do you pray? Are your prayers usually for your own needs or the needs of others?

(6:22, 23) Have you ever been insulted or excluded because of Jesus? If so, when? Were you later able to rejoice? Why?

(6:27-36) When have you been able to love your enemies? Has it been easier to love them or pray for them? Has one helped you to do the other? Explain. How has your love for enemies been a witness to others?

(6:43-49) What good fruit are you producing in Jesus' name? What words overflow out of what is in your heart?

What idea, verse, or phrase from this chapter can change your experience today?

Day 51
Luke 7

Background: One of Luke's purposes in writing his gospel is to show that Jesus message is not just for the Jews. The actions of Jesus witness to the fact that the love and mercy of God is for all people, whether Jew or Gentile, uneducated or educated, poor or rich.

(7:1-10) Describe the centurion in this story. What would cause this Roman soldier to turn to a Jewish faith healer for help? Why is Jesus amazed?

(7:11-17) Women in Jesus' day rarely worked and were not allowed to own property. The death of this widow's son would leave her without anyone to support her. What would Jesus' actions here mean for this woman? In what ways has Jesus rescued you?

(7:18-19) What question would you like to ask Jesus?

(7:36-38) Why did this woman "who was a sinner" love Jesus so much? Why do you love Jesus?

(7:39-50) What specific debt(s) has Jesus forgiven you? How has this caused your love for him to grow? How do you show your love for him?

What idea, verse, or phrase from this chapter can change your experience today?

Day 52
Luke 8

Background: It is important to Luke that his readers understand the divine power of Jesus. As with Mark's Gospel, this suggests that Luke's readers were citizens of the powerful Roman Empire. To convince these people that Jesus is God, Luke shows them the power and authority of Jesus.

Over what does Jesus demonstrate his divine authority in each passage?

(8:23-24)

(8:29)

(8:44)

(8:53-56)

(8:1-3) Are you surprised to see women prominently listed here along with the reference to the twelve apostles? Why or why not? What does this tell you about Jesus? How are these women involved in the ministry of Jesus? How do you support Jesus' ministry?

(8:19-21) Who does Jesus identify as his mother and brothers? Does Jesus see you like a mother or brother today? What part of God's word are you putting into practice?

(8:22-25) What were the disciples feeling before they woke Jesus? What happened to their faith? Have you ever lost your faith in Jesus?

What idea, verse, or phrase from this chapter can change your experience today?

Day 53
Luke 9

Background: The sending out of the twelve apostles to preach and teach and heal reveals something quite significant about the ministry of Jesus. The example he sets is that of training and equipping "Christ-centered" leaders to go out and do ministry directly with the people. Thus Jesus broadens the base for ministry so that many others receive God's love.

(9:1-9) Why does Jesus tell his apostles to take nothing with them on their missionary journeys? What possessions get in the way of the work to which Jesus has called you? What does this missionary effort teach about the role of congregations in the support of missionaries?

(9:10-17) Does it surprise you that the apostles, after their successful work of preaching, teaching and healing, lack the faith to feed the crowd as Jesus asks them? Why might that be? What important work have you done for Jesus? How has that affected your faith? What great thing is he asking you to do today?

(9:46-48) What is your definition of greatness? How well does that match the definition that Jesus gives? In what ways are you seeking to be the least rather than the greatest?

(9:57-62) What excuses do these people use to avoid Jesus' call to follow? What excuses do you have for not following Christ today?

What idea, verse, or phrase from this chapter can change your experience today?

Day 54
Luke 10

Background: Some ancient manuscripts record the number sent out in 10:1, 17 as seventy, while other say seventy-two. Seventy may be the more likely choice because the number seven represents perfection and when multiplied by ten represents many.

(10:1-20) Notice how Jesus has increased the number of those witnessing. Initially there were twelve apostles. How many are there now? How did he accomplish this? In what ways is your church seeking to enlarge its base for ministry and witness? How are you helping to grow the base for witness?

(10:20) What do you think is the meaning of this verse? Do you know that your name is written in heaven? How can you be sure?

(10:25-37) What is the question Jesus answers with this parable? What is Jesus' answer? Are you more often like those who pass by on the other side or like the one who stops to help? What keeps you from stopping? What can help you to help more often?

(10:38-42) If Jesus came to your home, are you more likely to respond in the fashion of Martha or Mary? What is the one thing that Jesus says is needed? When do you sit at the feet of the Lord? Thank Jesus that his good words will not be taken from you!

What idea, verse, or phrase from this chapter can change your experience today?

Day 55
Luke 11

Background: The teachings of Jesus are designed to accomplish several things in the lives of the listeners: (1) develop faith and understanding about the love of God, (2) encourage them in their walk of faith, and (3) prepare them to share the message with others.

(11:1) Why did Jesus teach this prayer to his followers? For what would you like to ask Jesus?

(11:2-3) A petition is something that is asked for in a prayer. What are the six petitions in the Lord's Prayer? For which of these do you most intensely pray?

(11:5-13) Why is the man successful in receiving bread from his friend? What does this teach you about prayer? Is there any reason not to ask God for something? What can you do to assure God's positive response to your prayers?

(11:23) Jesus says here that one can only be for Jesus or against Jesus; there is no in between. Are you for or against Jesus? What are you seeking to do in his name?

(11:37-54) What is Jesus suggesting when he compares the Pharisees to the cup and dish? Where do you see this kind of hypocritical behavior today? Does your inner life reflect what you show to others when you come to worship God? Explain.

What idea, verse, or phrase from this chapter can change your experience today?

Day 56
Luke 12

Background: Blaspheming against the Holy Spirit (verse 10) is one of the more confusing or difficult to understand teachings of Christ. The implication is that the unforgivable sin is that of giving credit to Satan for that which the Holy Spirit accomplished.

(12:4-12) Of what worldly things are you afraid? Do the words of Jesus here comfort and encourage you? Why or why not?

(12:13-21) What are you storing up for the future? Would this be pleasing or disappointing to God? Explain. In what ways are you rich toward God?

(12:32-34) What are the dangers in being rich? Why do we need to give to the poor? What is the great treasure of your heart?

(12:35-40) In what ways are waiting expectantly for the master to return?

(12:42-48) When have you been given much by God? For what has God asked in return?

(12:57-59) To what voices do you listen when you must make a decision? Which voices carry the greatest weight in your decision-making?

What idea, verse, or phrase from this chapter can change your experience today?

Day 57
Luke 13

Background: In Jesus' day, it was common to assume that misfortune would only come to those who were extremely sinful. In the beginning of this chapter, Jesus stresses that all are sinners who are in need of repentance.

(13:6-9) Are you producing fruit for the Lord? If so, what? If not, has God given you ample opportunity to do so? How can you help to cultivate others so that they too might bear good fruit?

(13:10-17) Why do the religious leaders become so angry when Jesus heals on the Sabbath? Whose power and authority does Jesus threaten today?

(13:18-20) What is Jesus saying here about the kingdom of God? How does this teaching make you feel? Why?

(13:22-30) In what ways today are people trying to enter heaven without going through the narrow door of faith in Jesus? How are you seeking to go through that door? What path does Jesus recommend for entering this door (verse 30)?

(13:31-35) Jesus laments for Jerusalem, which so often killed the messengers of God. For what or whom would Jesus lament today?

What idea, verse, or phrase from this chapter can change your experience today?

Day 58
Luke 14

Background: Much of Jesus' teaching is designed to encourage action and witness on the part of his followers. Faith is enough for salvation, but actions show gratitude for and commitment to God's love.

(14:1-11) Do you tend to think of yourself as being worthy of an important place or a lesser place? How does Jesus encourage us to think about ourselves? When have you exalted yourself and been humbled? When have you been exalted after humbling yourself?

(14:12-14) What does Jesus say our attitude should be toward those who can give little or nothing? Who does your congregation seek to invite "to the banquet"? When was the last time you invited someone who could not repay doing something for you?

(14:15-24) Who are those who will not enter the kingdom of God? What excuses have you heard from those who are choosing not to attend? How can you help to invite them in?

(14:25) The word hate is used comparatively here to show that one must love Jesus more than all others. Who has been most difficult for you to "hate" in order to put Jesus first?

(14:34-35) How are you keeping your "saltiness" in the faith? How are you helping others to stay "salty"?

What idea, verse, or phrase from this chapter can change your experience today?

Day 59
Luke 15

Background: Jesus' use of parables made his teachings more memorable, although they often included hidden meanings needing further explanation. These hidden meanings challenged those who were truly interested to return for further instruction. It also hid certain truths from unbelievers who might use them against Jesus.

Give a name to each of these parables:

(15:3-7)

(15:8-10)

(15:11-32)

(15:1-2) What difference do you note between the reaction of the Pharisees and teachers of the law and the reaction of those who found what was lost (15:7, 10, 23)?

(15:11-24) When have you felt like the younger son in this parable? How did you experience God's welcoming love? Thank God for that forgiveness and love. How have you shared that love with others?

(15:25-32) When have you felt like the older brother? Would those feelings change if you recognized the lost one as sister or brother? Explain. What kind of celebration would you plan for one who was lost?

What idea, verse, or phrase from this chapter can change your experience today?

Day 60
Luke 16

Background: It seems odd that Jesus would use an apparently dishonest manager as an example for his followers (16:1-8). Interpreters suspect that the manager may have been erasing interest payments that his master did not have the right to charge.

(16:1-9) How are you using your worldly wealth? Do you see it as a tool to make friends for Jesus? Why or why not? How might you use your wealth more shrewdly?

(16:10-12) With what true riches has God entrusted you? How are you using them?

(16:16-18) How does Jesus say the people are responding to the good news of the kingdom of God? How are you seeking to enter the kingdom? Jesus says here that heaven and earth will pass away before keeping the law (good works) will achieve one's salvation.

(16:19-31) Do you know anyone who has intentionally rejected the testimony of Scripture? Pray that this person's mind might be opened to the good news of the resurrection of Jesus.

What idea, verse, or phrase from this chapter can change your experience today?

Day 61
Luke 17

Background: The need for faith is a core theme in Luke's gospel. It is very important to Luke that his readers understand that it is faith in Jesus that is necessary for salvation. Furthermore, if you believe in Jesus, nothing in this earthly existence need be feared.

(17:1-2) Who are those today who intentionally cause others to sin?

(17:3-5) What instructions does Jesus give us here? How will you deal with the sins of another? How will you receive another who points out your sins? Is this something for which you will need more faith? Why or why not?

(17:7-10) What work has the Lord God assigned you to do? Have you sought to do it faithfully? What praise do you deserve from God for your work? Are you ready to do more? Explain.

(17:11-19) Why might the nine lepers have failed to return to thank Jesus? For what have you forgotten to thank God? Take time to do so now.

(17:20-37) What things in your earthly life would be most difficult to give up? Are these things more important than life eternal with God?

What idea, verse, or phrase from this chapter can change your experience today?

Day 62
Luke 18

Background: Luke continues to stress the importance of prayer in this chapter. Prayer is one of the most valuable tools for keeping one's faith strong and healthy.

(18:1-8) Why does this widow finally receive the judgment she desires? If an unjust God gives in to the persistent pleas of a widow, how will our just God respond to our requests? What kind of faith will Christ find in the world when he returns? What kind of faith will Christ find in you?

(18:9-14) What motivates the Pharisee in his prayer? What motivates the tax collector? To which of these are your prayers more similar?

(18:15-17) What are the qualities of children that Jesus would value in all his followers? Which of these qualities do you possess?

(18:18-29) What differences do you see between the rich young ruler and the children in the previous story? How would childlike faith help this man to do what Jesus tells him?

(18:35-43) Why would the crowd have tried to send this man away from Jesus? Why might Jesus have asked such an obvious question of this blind man? Are you this direct in your requests of God? For what can you praise God today?

What idea, verse, or phrase from this chapter can change your experience today?

Day 63
Luke 19

Background: A pound equaled 100 drachmas, and one drachma was equal to about a day's wages. So the amount entrusted to each servant in the parable of the ten pounds was three months' wages.

(19:1-10) Describe Zacchaeus and how he must have felt about others at the beginning of this story. How did he feel about others at the end of the story? What caused this change? How has your contact with Jesus changed you?

(19:11-27) In what ways does Jesus fit the description of the nobleman in this parable? Who are the servants to whom he has entrusted his affairs? What has Jesus given to you? Have you been a good servant with what the nobleman has given you? Explain.

(19:41-44) Why is Jesus moved to tears? What does this tell you about his feelings regarding the coming judgment? Does anything about the condition of the world today move you to tears? Why or why not?

(19:45-48) Why would the religious leaders be upset at Jesus for chasing the sellers and moneylenders out of the temple? Why does it upset Jesus that they are there? In what ways are churches today houses of prayer? In what ways are they a "den of robbers"?

What idea, verse, or phrase from this chapter can change your experience today?

Day 64
Luke 20

Background: The events beginning in this chapter (ending in 21:36) all occurred on Tuesday of the week of Jesus' death. Mark's parallel account helps us to know that the triumphal entry occurred on Sunday and the cleansing of the temple on Monday.

(20:1-8) Here the religious leaders are challenging Jesus' authority to cleanse the temple. Has God given you authority to change what is wrong in God's church? If so, from where does this authority come?

(20:9-16) Who in this parable is the owner? The tenants? The slaves? The son? In what ways have you welcomed the messengers God has sent to you? In what ways have you rejected them?

(20:20) Why are the religious leaders so desperate to get rid of Jesus? Is their concern for themselves or for the people? Explain.

(20:21-26) How do church and state come into conflict today? To whom should you answer in these situations?

(20:27-39) What does it mean to you that our God is the God of the living? What does this suggest about the resurrection of the dead?

What idea, verse, or phrase from this chapter can change your experience today?

Day 65
Luke 21

Background: The temple treasury was a series of containers shaped like inverted megaphones into which worshipers could drop their donations. This money was to be used for the poor and for widows who had no one to provide for them.

(21:1-4) Why might this poor widow have been so willing to give out of her poverty? How does 2 Corinthians 8:12 help explain Jesus' reaction to her gift? Do you give out of your poverty or out of your abundance? Explain.

(21:5-19) What signs does Jesus say will precede the end of the age? What are the promises of verses 15 and 19?

(21:20-32) Jesus' warnings here refer to the future destruction of the city and the temple in Jerusalem in 70 A.D. Is there a parallel for us with regard to the end of the world? Explain.

(21:34-38) Does this warning cause you to rethink any of the choices you are currently making in your life? What emotions do you feel as you contemplate one day having to stand before Christ?

What idea, verse, or phrase from this chapter can change your experience today?

Day 66
Luke 22

Background: Luke records that as Jesus prayed, his sweat fell like drops of blood. The good doctor is reporting a medical condition called hematidrosis. Under extreme stress, capillaries in the forehead actually burst, causing blood to mix with perspiration.

(22:1-6) What kinds of behaviors or motives might have made Judas more susceptible to the tempting of Satan? How are you working to stay committed to Christ, so as to resist the devil's invitations?

(22:7-20) Read Exodus 12:1-28. How does Jesus fit the description of the Passover lamb? Indeed, he is the Lamb of God who takes away the sins of the world! With what words does Jesus suggest that this meal be celebrated with others?

(22:31-34) When has overconfidence gotten you into trouble? Who knows us better—God or ourselves? How does that make you feel?

(22:39-46) What emotions does Jesus experience in the garden? When have you experienced similar emotions? What made it difficult for the disciples to pray with Jesus? What things interfere with your prayer life?

(22:47-53) Why would Jesus heal the high priest's servant when he showed no evidence of faith? Do you think the slave was changed by this event? Explain.

What idea, verse, or phrase from this chapter can change your experience today?

Day 67
Luke 23

Background: The charges brought against Jesus were serious in the eyes of the Roman Empire, but were entirely untrue. Jesus never opposed paying taxes (see 20:25), and while he claimed to be the Christ or Savior, this was not a political issue that would threaten Rome.

(23:1-2) What lies or false teachings have you heard attributed to Jesus? When have you stood up in defense of Jesus?

(23:6-12) When have you tried to send Jesus off somewhere else so you would not have to face his truth? How did Jesus return to confront you again? Are you grateful for his persistence?

(23:26) How would your life be changed if you had been enlisted to carry the cross of Jesus?

(23:46) In what situations have you turned your life over to your heavenly Father? How did God respond to your faith?

(23:47) What things did the centurion witness during Jesus' crucifixion that impressed him enough to make this statement? What things about Jesus' death most impress you? What statement do you wish to publicly make about Jesus?

What idea, verse, or phrase from this chapter can change your experience today?

Day 68
Luke 24

Background: During the 40 days following Jesus' resurrection, he appeared to more than 500 people on no fewer than 11 occasions. The broadness of these appearances makes it very difficult to support claims of mass hallucinations, as some skeptics have claimed.

(24:1-12) How would you have reacted to the discovery made by the women on that Easter morning? What would you have told the disciples? Have you ever shared the message that Christ is alive today? How have others reacted?

(24:13-35) Does it surprise you that the disciples did not recognize Jesus? Why or why not? Why is it significant that they recognized Jesus in the breaking of the bread? Are you aware of the presence of Jesus in the sharing of the bread in worship? In what ways?

(24:36) In what new way do you understand this traditional greeting in light of the resurrection? What peace does Jesus give to you because of the resurrection?

(24:45-49) How much easier is it to understand the teachings of Jesus on this side of the resurrection?

(24:50-53) How has Jesus blessed you? Thank him for these things!

What idea, verse, or phrase from this chapter can change your experience today?

Day 69
John 1

Background: Like the Gospels of Matthew and Luke, John includes a Christmas story (John 1:1-14). John's nativity story, though, is very different for the purpose of emphasizing the divine nature of Jesus.

(1:1-5) Read the first chapter of Genesis. What parallels do you find between Genesis and the beginning of John's Gospel? What things does John tell you that are supported by Genesis?

(1:10-14) Who is the Word who became flesh? For what reason did the Word become flesh? Have you believed in his name? What has that meant for you?

(1:15-36) In what ways does John the baptizer point away from himself and toward Jesus? How have you done the same?

(1:38) How do you answer Jesus' question?

(1:42) The name Peter means "rock." This name reflected not who Simon was but whom, by God's grace, he would become. Who or what, by God's grace, are you becoming?

What idea, verse, or phrase from this chapter can change your experience today?

Day 70
John 2

Background: We know little about the wedding customs of Jesus' day. It seems clear, though, that the wedding feast might go on for as long as a week. To fail to be a proper host was a serious offense to the guests. Jesus provides excellent hospitality to the guests and spares the host tremendous embarrassment.

(2:1-11) Does Jesus' response to his mother surprise you? Why or why not? Why did Mary turn to Jesus in this situation? When do you turn to Jesus and what do you expect him to do?

(2:11) John often refers to the miracles of Jesus as signs (or miraculous signs). Why would John refer to them in this way?

(2:12-17) Matthew, Mark, and Luke indicate that the cleansing of the temple occurred toward the end of Jesus' ministry. What significance would it have at the end? What significance would it have here? Does the difference between the gospels cause any issues of faith for you? Explain.

(2:18-22) To what do the people think Jesus is referring? To what is Jesus actually referring? Why did the disciples not understand what Jesus meant until after his resurrection? What is easier for you to believe on this side of the cross?

What idea, verse, or phrase from this chapter can change your experience today?

Day 71
John 3

Background: John's is the last of the four gospels written. Scholars believe that one of his reasons for writing was to correct details in the other three gospels. John has good reason to do this.

(3:1-2) Why would Nicodemus come to talk to Jesus in the dark of night? What does he know about Jesus?

(3:3-15) What does Jesus say to Nicodemus (and to us) about receiving eternal life? When were you born of water and the Spirit? Has your life been different since your "rebirth"? If so, how?

(3:16-18) Why did God send Jesus into the world? What promises are given to those who believe? Jesus speaks here of a continuing, lasting belief that carries through life. What are you doing to keep your faith strong?

(3:19-21) Who choose to live in darkness in today's world? How can you bring the light of God to them?

(3:27-30) What have your received from heaven? How have you made yourself less so that Jesus can become greater? Has this given you joy?

What idea, verse, or phrase from this chapter can change your experience today?

Day 72
John 4

Background: Two things are odd about Jesus' conversation with the woman at the well. First, she was a Samaritan. Second, she came to the well at "the sixth hour"—about noon. Samaritans were half Jew, half Gentiles and were looked down upon by "pure" Jews. Coming to the well at noon suggested that she was an outcast to the other women who would come at an earlier, cooler hour.

(4:1-4) Was it success or failure that led to Jesus leaving the region of Judea? Why would this result cause him to leave?

(4:7-26) Why does the Samaritan woman misunderstand Jesus at first? How is this conversation like and unlike Jesus' conversation with Nicodemus in John 3? What do these conversations teach you about talking to others about Jesus?

(4:27-30, 39-42) What is the process of the growth in faith of the town's people? What do the actions of the woman and the people of the town teach you about witnessing for Christ? How can you have a part in bringing others to Jesus?

(4:43-54) Why does the official take Jesus at his word and return home? What promise has Jesus made to you that you took on faith? What was the result?

What idea, verse, or phrase from this chapter can change your experience today?

Day 73
John 5

Background: In Jesus' day, pools like the one at Bethzatha (also recorded as Bethesda and Bethsaida) were believed to have curative powers. When the water bubbled (verse 7), those who were sick would be placed in the water for healing.

(5:1-9) Why do you think Jesus asks the man the question in verse 6? Can you imagine someone not wanting to be well? Explain. Have you ever chosen to stay in your current situation without seeking to be healed? Consider not just physical healing but other kinds of healing.

(5:9-15) Does the response of the people to the man carrying his mat surprise you? Explain. What religious rules today get in the way of celebrating the good fortune that comes into people's lives? How does sin make our situation worse?

(5:16-18) When has the response of someone about her or his relationship with God angered you? Why?

(5:24) What does it mean to you that Jesus speaks of eternal life in the present tense? How have you receive eternal life as a present possession?

(5:39-40) Do you know anyone who is so involved in religious activities that he or she seems to miss the truth about Jesus? How can you help this person come to Jesus?

What idea, verse, or phrase from this chapter can change your experience today?

Day 74
John 6

Background: John records here that the Passover feast was near. John records at least three different Passovers during Jesus' ministry (2:23, 6:4, and 12:1). This helps us to know the number of years that Jesus' ministry lasted.

(6:1-15) What question does Jesus ask Philip? Why does he ask this? What does Andrew add to the conversation? How do you think these two felt after everyone had eaten and the leftovers were gathered? When has Jesus surprised you?

(6:16-21) In the midst of what storms has Jesus come to you? How did you know it was him? How did you receive Christ?

(6:22-24) How far have you gone to find Jesus?

(6:28-29) Are you surprised by the answer Jesus gives to the crowd? Why or why not? How does this "work," called for by God, lead to other works? To what works has the "work of God" led you?

(6:44-45, 65) What role can you have in your salvation? How does this make you feel?

What idea, verse, or phrase from this chapter can change your experience today?

Day 75
John 7

Background: The Feast of Tabernacles was one of the most important celebrations in the life of the Jews. Similar to our celebration of Thanksgiving, it celebrated the end of harvest time and gave thanks for God's goodness to the Israelites during their exodus journey. The name came from the shelters the people built and lived in during the festival.

(7:1-5) Why would Jesus' brothers encourage him to go to the place where he was most likely to be arrested or killed? Why do family members or friends sometimes stand in the way of their loved ones having access to Jesus?

(7:6) Are you more in tune with God's time or your own? When have you had to wait for God's time to come?

(7:30) What power does Jesus show here? From where does that power come? In what situations might that power be available to you?

(7:37-38) What thirst has Jesus quenched for you? In what ways do the "living waters" of Jesus flow from within you? To whom does God want your living waters to flow?

(7:45-52) What does Nicodemus risk by his response to the Pharisees? What risks have you taken on behalf of Jesus?

What idea, verse, or phrase from this chapter can change your experience today?

Day 76
John 8

Background: In the last chapter and this one, John reports the strong opposition to Jesus. In this section, John has gathered and answered the arguments of his day against Jesus being the Messiah.

(8:2-11) Who has the power at the beginning of this event? At what points does the power shift? How does Jesus empower the powerless in this story? Who are the powerless today? How is Jesus sending you to empower them?

(8:12) Where is Jesus' light shining today? In what dark places is it most needed? How are you walking in the light?

(8:31-36) How will others know that you are one of Jesus' disciples? What promise does Jesus make to those who follow him? Who will be most glad to hear this good news?

(8:42-47) What warning does this passage give? Do you belong to God? What do you hear God saying to you?

(8:58) Why is it significant that Jesus says, "I am!" rather than "I was"? What comfort does this statement give you?

What idea, verse, or phrase from this chapter can change your experience today?

Day 77
John 9

Background: The miracle of giving sight to the blind was foretold as a sign of the Messiah (Isaiah 29:18; 35:5; 42:7). John records several occurrences of this type of miracle to support his claim that Jesus is the predicted Savior of the world.

(9:1-7) When did a crisis in your life turn out to be an opportunity for the work of God to be displayed? Who does Jesus say must be about the work of God?

(9:8-34) How does the testimony of the man Jesus healed change during these various questionings? How has your witnessing for Jesus grown stronger over time?

(9:8-34) What are the Pharisees saying about Jesus when they refer to him as "a sinner"? What are they saying about themselves? What things make it difficult for people today to rejoice and give glory to God when God blesses someone?

(9:39-41) Who are the spiritually blind in the world today? What causes their blindness? How can Jesus heal those who are spiritually blind?

(9:1-41) What first opened this man's heart to hear about Jesus? What direction does this give you about the process of guiding people to faith in Jesus? What role can you play in bringing someone to faith?

What idea, verse, or phrase from this chapter can change your experience today?

Day 78
John 10

Background: A heresy that circulated during John's day was that Jesus was not really from God but instead had been adopted by God at his baptism. One of John's purposes in writing this gospel is to combat this false teaching.

(10:1-6) Is your image of a shepherd that of one who drives the sheep or that of one who leads the sheep? How does Jesus describe the shepherd? How do you feel about this description? Do you know the Shepherd's voice?

(10:7-18) In what ways does Jesus describe himself here? Which image do you prefer and why? How does Jesus distinguish between a good shepherd and a hired hand? What proves that Jesus is the Good Shepherd?

(10:16) To whom might Jesus be referring when he speaks of "other sheep"?

(10:22-30) How did Jesus' life answer the question of the Jews? Why do they still not believe? Who are Jesus' sheep? What does Jesus promise to his sheep?

(10:30-39) Does it surprise you that after all they had seen and heard, the Jews considered Jesus' statement in verse 30 to be blasphemy? Explain. What does it tell you that Jesus was able to escape here but was arrested later?

What idea, verse, or phrase from this chapter can change your experience today?

Day 79
John 11

Background: Another of John's goals is to inspire faith in his readers (see 20:31). John repeatedly highlights events and teachings on the part of Jesus that shows him to be the one through whom we receive eternal life and the other gifts of God.

(11:1-6) Why does Jesus delay in going to see his sick friend? Under whose direction or timing does Jesus move? In what situations today do you need to surrender to God's timing? Is this easy or difficult? Why?

(11:7-16) What does Thomas's comment reflect about himself? How far will you travel with Jesus?

(11:25-26) What does this promise mean for you? How would you answer Jesus' question?

(11:32-37) What emotions does Jesus show? What does it mean for you that Jesus experiences these kinds of feelings?

(11:38-44) What causes Martha to overcome her doubts? What does she receive for her faith? What have you received from Jesus for your faith?

What idea, verse, or phrase from this chapter can change your experience today?

Day 80
John 12

Background: Mary's act of anointing Jesus was both costly and unusual. Nard, both a plant and the fragrant oil from it, was quite expensive. Normally, the oil was poured over the head to anoint—and a respectable woman did not undo her hair in public. Mary's devotion to Jesus knew no boundaries.

(12:1-8) What boundaries have you crossed to show your devotion to Jesus? How have you given honor to him? Consider Jesus' words in verse 8 in light of Matthew 25:34-40. How will you show your devotion to Jesus by serving the least?

(12:23-26) How does Jesus' death explain his illustration of the grain of wheat? What is most difficult for you to "hate" in order that your love for God is great by comparison? How has God honored you for your service to Jesus?

(12:28) Where is God's name glorified today? How do you seek to give glory to God's name?

(12:35-36) Do you think our world is becoming a darker place? Explain. What places in the world are most in need of the light of Jesus?

(12:42-43) When is the praise of people more important to you than the praise of God?

What idea, verse, or phrase from this chapter can change your experience today?

Day 81
John 13

Background: John records more of what happened in the upper room than does any other gospel writer. It is odd, though, that he makes no mention of the Lord's Supper. As you read this chapter and the next, note the emphasis Jesus places on love.

(13:1-17) What lesson does Jesus the teacher give to his followers? Which would you prefer—to wash the feet of another or to have your feet washed? Why? To whom will you do an act of humble service this week?

(13:6-10) How does Simon Peter show humility? How does he show pride? Has Jesus washed you? If so, when? What part of your life needs to be washed today? Ask Jesus to make you completely clean!

(13:30) How does Jesus transfer his earthly mission to his followers? What is that mission? How have you sought to carry it out?

(13:21-30) What might have made Judas more open to the temptations of Satan? When has Satan led you to betray Jesus? How do you protect yourself against his tempting today?

(13:34-35) When is this command difficult for you to follow? What reasons does Jesus give us for following this command? When has your act of love for another witnessed to your discipleship for Jesus?

What idea, verse, or phrase from this chapter can change your experience today?

Day 82
John 14

Background: John's understanding of the teachings of Jesus is best summed up in this chapter. Through John's Gospel, we come to understand that love for God and keeping Jesus' commands go hand in hand.

(13:36-14:14) What are the questions that Simon Peter, Thomas, and Philip ask? How does Jesus answer these questions?

(14:1-4) What promise does Jesus make here? What hope does this give you? Thank Jesus for preparing a place in his kingdom for you!

(14:13-14) What is Jesus' promise in these verses? What requirement does Jesus make for these requests? Have your requests always met this requirement? Explain. What has been the result of your requests?

(14:15-21) Look at 4:23-24, 14:6, and 14:17. What is common to all three persons of the Trinity? What truth does the Spirit bring? How do we show our love for God?

(14:27) What kind of peace is Jesus speaking about? Can we achieve this kind of peace on our own? Explain.

What idea, verse, or phrase from this chapter can change your experience today?

Day 83
John 15

Background: John uses seven "I am" statements to describe Jesus: "I am the bread of life" (6:35); "the light of the world" (8:12, 9:5); "the gate" (10:7, 9); "the good shepherd" (10:11, 14); "the resurrection and the life" (11:25); "the way, the truth, and the life" (14:6); and "the vine" (15:1, 5). Recall also how God responded to Moses in Exodus 3:14.

(15:1-4) Why does Jesus use the word true here? When have you been "pruned" to bear more fruit? How do you "remain" in Jesus?

(15:5-8) What fruit specifically are you bearing as a branch of Christ? When have you seen someone wither apart from the vine? How can you reconnect this person to the vine?

(15:9-17) What does Jesus say is the key to "remaining" in him? What is the process for remaining in Jesus? Again, what is the command that Jesus gives? Of what significance is it to you that Jesus calls you friend?

(15:16) In what way does this verse say we come into relationship to Jesus? Do you know others who view this process differently? How do they see it? To what does this process lead us?

(15:18-25) What caution does Jesus give? What guarantee? Between what must we choose? Which one did you choose?

What idea, verse, or phrase from this chapter can change your experience today?

Day 84
John 16

Background: As you read verses 14 through 16, you may feel a sense of urgency in the words of Jesus. He understands that his earthly ministry is under the control of God's time frame. Thus, he must prepare his followers to carry on the mission of God in the world.

(16:1-4) When have you seen religious people put out of the place of worship those who did not conform to their idea of the church? How can you show hospitality to those who are not like others at your church?

(16:5-11) What are the three ways that the Holy Spirit will "condemn" the world? Explain how the Holy Spirit does each of these things in your life.

(16:12-16) What things does this passage say the Holy Spirit will do? How is this good news?

(16:23-28) To whom does Jesus say we should pray? How should we pray?

(16:33) What contrasts does Jesus make in this verse? What kind of trouble does the world give? What kind of peace does Jesus offer?

What idea, verse, or phrase from this chapter can change your experience today?

Day 85
John 17

Background: This chapter is known as Jesus' high priestly prayer. It is the longest of any prayer by Jesus in the gospels. The role of the high priest was to intercede or pray on behalf of the people.

(17:1-5) For whom does Jesus pray in this section? Does this surprise you? Explain. When you pray for yourself, for what do you ask?

(17:6-19) For whom does Jesus pray in this section? What does Jesus ask the Father to do for them? What does it mean to be "in the world" but not "of the world"?

(17:17-19) To "sanctify" means to "make holy," "make special," or "set apart." How does the truth make one holy or special? For what have Jesus' disciples been set apart?

(17:20-26) For whom does Jesus pray here? What does Jesus request for them?

(17:23) What is it that can unite Jesus' followers? What usually keeps his followers divided?

What idea, verse, or phrase from this chapter can change your experience today?

Day 86
John 18

Background: At Jesus' arrest, John records a threefold "I am" (verses 5, 6, and 8). As does his other "I am" statements, this echoes the divine identification made by God in the burning bush (Exodus 3:14). It also emphasizes the honesty of Jesus' responses.

(18:1-11) Why would the crowd have reacted the way they did in verse 6? With what does Jesus seem to primarily be concerned during this event? What does Jesus' response in verse 11 suggest that Simon Peter's actions are trying to do?

(18:19-24) What do you notice about Jesus' attitude during this questioning? What is the attitude of those questioning him?

(18:25-27) To whom is it easy to confess your allegiance to Jesus? To whom is it difficult? Do you find it remarkable that Jesus was able to predict (John 13:38) this event in Simon Peter's life? Explain. What warnings has Jesus given you? Have you heeded them? Why or why not?

(18:28-40) What irony do you find in Pilate's question to Jesus in verse 38? How would you answer Pilate's question? On which side of truth is Pilate? On which side of truth are you? Explain.

What idea, verse, or phrase from this chapter can change your experience today?

Day 87
John 19

Background: A cross for execution might be shaped like a T, an X, a Y, or an I, as well as the form we usually see. As part of his punishment, a condemned man would have to carry part of his cross, usually the crossbeam to the place of execution outside of the city.

(19:1-16) What do Jesus' words to Pilate in verse 11 suggest about public officials? What, then, should be the motivation of public officials in their work? Why should we be supportive of governmental leaders? When should we not?

(19:25-27) To whom does Jesus give the responsibility for caring for his mother? What does this teach us about Christian community? For whom has Jesus given you responsibility within the body of Christ? How have you taken that person "into your home"?

(19:28-30) What was finished? What does it suggest to you that Jesus "gave up" his spirit?

(19:35) What have you witnessed with regard to Jesus? How are you giving testimony to this?

(19:38-42) What might have given Joseph and Nicodemus the courage to openly serve Jesus in this way? Why now when he was dead rather than when he was alive?

What idea, verse, or phrase from this chapter can change your experience today?

Day 88
John 20

Background: There are 11 occasions recorded within the four gospels, Acts, and 1 Corinthians on which Jesus physically appeared following his death and resurrection. Several of these are in two or more locations in Scripture. In all, Jesus appeared to more than 500 people after he rose.

(20:1-9) Despite his denials of knowing Jesus, Simon Peter was still considered the leader of the disciples. What does this teach you about the potential role of those who sometimes fail Jesus? What does this say to you?

(20:10-18) What emotions do you find in Mary in this narrative? Which of these emotions have you experienced with regard to Jesus and when? What is the importance of Jesus' words, "my Father and your Father...my God and your God"?

(20:19-23) Read Genesis 2:7. What did the first human being receive when God "breathed" into him? What do Jesus' disciples receive when he breathes upon them? What responsibilities come with this breath?

(20:24-31) What is John's purpose in writing this gospel? What have you seen that has helped you to believe? What have you seen because you believed? Try to share that with another person this week so that she or he may believe and have life in Jesus' name!

What idea, verse, or phrase from this chapter can change your experience today?

Day 89
John 21

Background: John's gospel makes several references to "the disciple whom Jesus loved." It is generally accepted that this is how John referred to himself in certain instances. It does not mean that Jesus did not love the other followers. Rather, it suggests a special relationship between Jesus and John. In closing his gospel, John gives final support for the belief that he is the author.

(21:1-11) Read Luke 5:1-11. What similarities do you see between these two narratives? What differences? How are repeated activities helpful in our recognition of Jesus? How does variety broaden our experiences with Jesus?

(21:12-13) List some of the other times in Scripture where a meal is shared. How are meals meaningful for the Christian community today?

(21:15-19) Why might Jesus have asked three times if Simon Peter loved him? What responsibility does Jesus give to Simon Peter because of his commitment to Jesus? What responsibilities have Jesus given you because of your love for him?

(21:19-23) What command does Jesus twice give to Simon Peter? What do Jesus' words in verse 22 suggest to us? When is it appropriate to be concerned about God's plans for another? When is it not?

What idea, verse, or phrase from this chapter can change your experience today?

Day 90
Acts 1

Background: The book of Acts is sometimes called the Acts of the Apostles because it is a history of the work of the apostles after Jesus ascended into heaven. A better name for this book might be the Acts of the Holy Spirit. Take note of how often the Holy Spirit is mentioned in each chapter.

(1:1) To whom is this book written? Read Luke 1:1-3. Who is the author of this book?

(1:1-5) Over how long a period of time did Jesus appear to his followers? What is important about eating with them? What does he promise to them?

(1:6-11) What do both verse 6 and verse 11 suggest about the disciples' understanding of who Jesus is and what his mission is? According to verse 8, what is their mission? What will be the driving force for that mission?

(1:12-26) What do the disciples do when they return to Jerusalem? For what might they have been praying? What decision does their praying lead them to make? What qualifications do they look for in a replacement for Judas? What does this process teach you about receiving and following God's vision?

What idea, verse, or phrase from this chapter can change your experience today?

Day 91
Acts 2

Background: Originally a Jewish holiday, Pentecost is the fiftieth day after the Sabbath of Passover week. Pentecost, for Christians, is the third great festival of the church year. Christmas celebrates God the creator becoming human; Easter celebrates God the Savior's victory over death; and Pentecost is the celebration of God the Spirit who gives faith and sends the church out in mission.

(2:1-13) What might Jesus' followers have been doing to make themselves open to the coming of the Holy Spirit? How do you make yourself open to the Spirit's presence? When has the Spirit enabled you to speak the "language" of another in order to share the good news of Jesus?

(2:14-21) What does the prophet Joel say will happen when the Holy Spirit comes? How does the Day of Pentecost fulfill this prophecy?

(2:36-41) How do the people respond to Peter's sermon about Jesus? What does Peter tell them? What is promised to them? To whom is this promise available?

(2:42-47) This passage (along with 4:32-35) describes the "golden age of the church." What are the characteristics and practices of the church during this period? What is the result of these activities? Which of these are present in your church? Which are missing?

What idea, verse, or phrase from this chapter can change your experience today?

Day 92
Acts 3

Background: Acts is an orderly account of the first 30 years or so of the Christian church. The Spirit directs the mission of the church, the spreading of the gospel of Jesus. Recall from Acts 2 that this mission began in a single room. Be aware of how it moves into all corners of the world!

(3:1-10) By what authority does Peter accomplish this miracle? Do you think the man was grateful for what he received? Explain. How might this encounter with the power of Jesus change his life? How has the power of Jesus changed your life?

(3:11-16) To whom does Peter give the credit for the healing miracle? For what can you witness in the name of Jesus?

(3:17-20) What does Peter tell his listeners to do? What promise is made to those who do so?

(3:22-23) How does Jesus fulfill the prophecy made by Moses?

(3:24) How does Jesus fulfill Samuel's prophecy of a great kingdom coming from the house of David?

(3:25-26) How does Jesus fulfill God's covenant or promise to Abraham?

What idea, verse, or phrase from this chapter can change your experience today?

Day 93
Acts 4

Background: One of the most remarkable things in Acts is the large numbers of people converted to Christianity in a very short time. In 2:41, on Pentecost, about three thousand became Christians. In 4:5 about two thousand more believe. Look also at 5:14 and 6:7. These numbers reflect only men, so the total conversions were likely much higher!

(4:8-12) The words healed in verse 10 and saved in verse 12 are actually the same word in the original Greek. Comment on the meanings of these two words with regard to the power of Jesus. How has Jesus provided you with power for healing and for salvation?

(4:13) What do you think gave Peter and John the boldness and courage to speak in Jesus' name in such a moving fashion?

(4:23-37) What things do the believers include in their prayer? Do they ask for their situation to be changed or for change in themselves? Why might they have asked for this?

(4:32-36) What behaviors are present in this Christian community? Which of these are present in your church? In your own life?

(4:36-37) Speculate on why Joseph might have been given the name "son of encouragement." Watch for his behaviors in future chapters.

What idea, verse, or phrase from this chapter can change your experience today?

Day 94
Acts 5

Background: Acts 5:11 uses the word church to describe the community of Christian believers. This is the first use of the term in the Bible. "Church" can be used to refer to the local church or to the church throughout the world.

(5:1-11) How was the behavior of Ananias and Sapphira different than that of Barnabas in 4:37? Of what sin were they guilty toward the Holy Spirit? Can you think of a time when guilt has made someone ill? What might have been the result here if these two had successfully deceived the Holy Spirit?

(5:12-16) Why did people bring the sick to places where the disciples might minister to them? When have you brought someone by name to be healed by the power of Jesus' name? Have you ever physically brought someone to be healed? Why or why not?

(5:17-20) What motivated the religious leaders to put the apostles in prison? Why would they feel that way? Can you think of similar circumstances today? Did the actions of those involved work to bring people to God or keep them from God? Explain.

(5:27-42) Have you ever made a statement of faith as the apostles did in verse 29? What was the outcome? What does Gamaliel's position reveal about him? What do the results of the disciples' efforts reveal based on Gamaliel's test?

What idea, verse, or phrase from this chapter can change your experience today?

Day 95
Acts 6

Background: The laying on of hands (verse 6) was done for healing, blessing, commissioning, and imparting spiritual gifts.

(6:1-6) What qualities were sought in the selection of seven men to be deacons (literally "table waiters")? Why would these qualities be important? Why was the selection of Nicolas from Antioch important?

(6:7) What was the result of the selection of deacons to relieve some of the responsibilities of the apostles? What does this teach you? How does this happen in your church?

(6:8) What is surprising about Stephen performing these things? How do you explain this in light of verse 6?

(6:9-10) Do the qualities sought in the first seven deacons make more sense now? Explain.

(6:11-15) How is Stephen's trial before the Sanhedrin like that of Jesus (see Mark 14:53-65)? How do you explain Stephen's appearance in verse 15?

What idea, verse, or phrase from this chapter can change your experience today?

Day 96
Acts 7

Background: One of Luke's purposes in writing Acts was to provide a document that would witness to both Jews and Gentiles the good news of Jesus. It shows how the early Christian church dealt with both pagan and Jewish thought.

(7:1-47) To whom is Stephen speaking? How does this explain the information he shares? What common theme runs though his narrative?

(7:48-50) To what charge is Stephen answering (see Acts 6:13-14)? What is Stephen saying in this passage with regard to this charge?

(7:51-53) Circumcision was an act through which a Jewish boy was consecrated to God. What is Stephen saying about his accusers here?

(7:54-60) What does Stephen's vision suggest about his testimony? How does Stephen's faith help him through this persecution? Explain how Stephen could ask for forgiveness for his killers.

(7:58, 8:1) Luke introduces Saul at this point in his second book. What role does Saul play in the death of Stephen? Pay attention to Saul's history as this book continues.

What idea, verse, or phrase from this chapter can change your experience today?

Day 97
Acts 8

Background: The development of new Christian leaders is essential to the continued growth of the church. Philip, who was first chosen to be one of the original seven deacons (Acts 6:5), now shares the role of evangelist along with Peter and the others.

(8:1-4) How does the Holy Spirit turn the persecution of the Christian church into an opportunity for the church to continue to grow? When in your life has God taken a negative event and brought positive things from it?

(8:5-8) Does it surprise you that Philip the deacon is now Philip the evangelist? Why or why not? When has God moved you from one role in the church to another?

(8:9-25) Give names to the stages in Simon's conversion to the Christian faith. What other stages can you name in faith development? In what stage are you?

(8:26-40) Why does the Spirit tell Philip to stay near the Ethiopian's chariot? Do you feel able to answer the questions of others about the Bible? What can you do to feel prepared? How knowledgeable do you think you need to be? What role does the Spirit play in equipping you to answer the faith questions of others?

What idea, verse, or phrase from this chapter can change your experience today?

Day 98
Acts 9

Background: The conversion of Saul the great Christian-killer into Paul the great Christian-maker (see 13:9) says much about what God can accomplish. Think of the many imperfect people throughout history who have been terrific witnesses for the faith. You could be, too!

(9:1-9) The name "the Way" is used several times in Acts to refer to the church. Why did the early church call itself this? (Look at John 14:6.) What does Jesus' question to Saul suggest about the relationship between Jesus and the church?

(9:10-19) If you were Ananias, how would you feel about being asked to go and minister to Saul? What difficult task has God placed before you? What great blessing does Jesus say will be accomplished through Saul? Keep this in mind as you seek to answer God's call!

(9:20-22) Why would Saul's history make people question the sincerity of his preaching? How would his past give strength to his message? What does this suggest to you as you consider witnessing to others about Jesus?

(9:23-31) Recall what the name Barnabas means (Acts 4:36). What other qualities do you think exist in Barnabas? What is the result of this act on the part of Barnabas (verse 31)?

What idea, verse, or phrase from this chapter can change your experience today?

Day 99
Acts 10

Background: An intimate relationship with a Gentile (non-Jew) was contrary to everything that Jews believed. Gentiles were "unclean" and association with them made a Jew unclean. Peter's vision in this chapter is the beginning of a shift in Christian outreach efforts from only Jews to include Gentiles as well.

(10:1-8) What qualities do you find in Cornelius? Does Cornelius seem to be lacking anything in his relationship with God? If so, what? Why might God want to bring Cornelius and Peter together?

(10:9-23) What practices in your life would be difficult to give up? Might any of them be barriers to sharing the good news of Jesus with others? What does Peter's vision teach you about God's priorities?

(10:34-43) What is the central point of Peter's message? What does this realization of Peter mean for the future of the church? Prior to this event Gentiles had to first become Jewish proselytes (converts) before they could become Christians. What now is the only requirement for the blessings of Jesus (verse 43)?

(10:44-48) This event is known as the "Gentile Pentecost." Why? Who is truly in charge of the spread of the gospel?

What idea, verse, or phrase from this chapter can change your experience today?

Day 100
Acts 11

Background: Even when a new way of reaching out results in many growing closer to God, there can still be resistance. Traditions ("We've never done it that way before!") and prejudices against folks who are different sadly can keep others from knowing Jesus.

(11:1-3) Notice that with regard to important matters, the apostles do not act alone (see also 15:4 and 15:22). How does your church handle major issues? Is this not a good way to make decisions? Explain. Why is the church concerned about Peter's behavior with regard to Cornelius (chapter 10)? What motivates this concern?

(11:4-18) What part of Peter's report do you think carries the most weight in persuading the Jerusalem church? Why do they rejoice and give praise to God? Over what things does your church celebrate?

(11:19-26) Into what places is the good news of Jesus now reaching? For what reason might the church have sent Barnabas to Antioch? For what reason might Barnabas have decided to bring Saul to Antioch? Based on this, what recommendation would you make for the relationship between churches today?

(11:27-30) The church now actively pursues a new ministry beyond evangelism and disciple-making. What is it? In what ways does your church participate in this form of ministry?

What idea, verse, or phrase from this chapter can change your experience today?

Day 101
Acts 12

Background: King Herod in this chapter is the grandson of Herod the Great who was visited by the wise men (Matthew 2:1). He also was a nephew of Herod Antipas, who had John the baptizer beheaded (Matthew 14:3-12) and tried Jesus (Luke 23:8-12).

(12:1-5) How does the church respond to Peter's arrest and imprisonment? For what situations does your church pray? How do your prayers help to build up the church?

(12:5-11) How does God answer the church's prayer? Why might Peter have thought this was only a vision or dream? What miracles has God performed in response to the prayers of your church?

(12:12-17) Why would the Christians be so surprised when Peter arrived, since this is for what they had been praying? Have you ever prayed for something that you really did not expect to happen? If so, why? Has God positively answered your prayers, even when you did not expect God to do so?

(12:18-24) What did Herod do that resulted in God's judgment upon him? Read Exodus 20:1-17. What commandment of God did Herod break?

What idea, verse, or phrase from this chapter can change your experience today?

Day 102
Acts 13

Background: John (Mark) may have been the young man in the linen cloth that followed Jesus to the Garden of Gethsemane (Mark 14:51). The early Christian church met often at the home of his mother, Mary (Acts 12:12). Barnabas and Saul (Paul) now take John Mark under their wing to develop him as a Christian leader.

(13:1-3) Describe the church in Antioch. What similarities do you find with your own church? What is different from your church?

(13:4-12) What two things convince the proconsul to believe in Jesus?

(13:13) Why might Paul now be listed first among this missionary group? How do you think Paul and Barnabas felt about John Mark leaving them to return to Jerusalem?

(13:16-25) What is Paul's theme in this part of his message? Why does he begin with this theme?

(13:26-41) What is Paul's central message in this part of his sermon?

(13:42-51) We are called to be faithful, not successful. In what ways do Paul and Barnabas exemplify this saying?

What idea, verse, or phrase from this chapter can change your experience today?

Day 103
Acts 14

Background: The Greeks worshiped many gods. Zeus was the greatest and most imposing of the gods. Hermes was the messenger of the gods. An ancient legend in Lystra said that Zeus and Hermes had once visited the city but were recognized only by an older couple. When Paul and Barnabas arrive, the city was apparently not going to risk ignoring the gods again.

(14:1-7) How does God support the efforts of Paul and Barnabas? How does God bless their efforts? How does God protect them?

(14:8-18) Why do the people of Lystra mistake Paul and Barnabas for gods? What are the "worthless things" to which Paul and Barnabas refer (verse 15)? How do they present God to these people?

(14:19-21) Why, after such treatment, would Paul and Barnabas continue to risk their lives for their message? How is their persistence rewarded? What risks have you taken for the gospel? How has God rewarded your efforts?

(14:22-28) What things do Paul and Barnabas now do for the churches they had previously established? How do churches today encourage and support one another?

What idea, verse, or phrase from this chapter can change your experience today?

Day 104
Acts 15

Background: This chapter marks the official change in the missionary efforts of the early Christian church. After the decision of the Jerusalem council, the church now actively pursues the conversion of all people to the Christian faith.

(15:1-5) Why was it so important for those who want to become new converts to be circumcised? What traditions in your church get in the way of bringing others to Jesus? Which is more important: traditions or the faith life of individuals? How can you work to change those traditions that interfere with spiritual growth?

(15:6-11) What does Peter say is the only necessary thing for salvation? How does the requirement of circumcision (or any human requirement) oppose God's grace in Jesus Christ?

(15:12-35) What practices does James (the brother of the Lord Jesus) suggest should be avoided by the new converts? Why might these practices hinder the spiritual growth of a Christian?

(15:36-41) Over what do Paul and Barnabas argue? How does Barnabas fulfill the meaning of his name (see Acts 4:36)? John Mark is considered the one who later writes the Gospel of Mark, the first gospel about Jesus. Were it not for Barnabas, this gospel might never have been written. Who can you take time to encourage today?

What idea, verse, or phrase from this chapter can change your experience today?

Day 105
Acts 16

Background: Timothy of Lystra is the same Timothy to whom Paul addresses the two biblical letters that bear his name. Not much is known of his Greek father, who was probably a non-believer. Timothy's grandmother Lois and his mother Eunice (2 Timothy 1:5), however, were both Christians.

(16:1-5) Why might Paul have wanted to take Timothy along? Why did Paul have Timothy circumcised? How are you working to train others in the faith so that they too might witness for our Lord?

(16:6-10) Note the change from "they" (verse 7) to "we" (verse 10). Who must have become a part of this missionary group? (Read Acts 1:1 and Luke 1:1-3 for help.) What direction does Paul receive from God on this part of the journey? How does God give you direction on your life journey?

(16:11-15) It was highly unusual in Paul's day for women to own businesses, and purple cloth was sold only to royalty and the very wealthy. What does this suggest to you about Lydia? What does Lydia do upon receiving the faith? How have you responded to receiving the faith?

(16:16-40) How do Paul and Silas deal with their imprisonment? How does God use this unfortunate incident to further the kingdom? What good things has God brought into your life out of misfortune?

What idea, verse, or phrase from this chapter can change your experience today?

Day 106
Acts 17

Background: Many of the letters found in the New Testament are letters from Paul to the churches he established on his missionary trips. Philippians is written to the Church at Philippi; Thessalonians to the Church at Thessalonica; Corinthians to the Church at Corinth, and so on.

(17:1-9) The phrase in verse 6 that is translated "These people who have been turning the world upside down" literally means "these world-turner-upside-downers." Is this a good description for Paul and Silas? Explain. How is the message of Jesus turning the world upside down today? How are you helping?

(17:10-15) What do the Beroeans do to test the message of Paul? In what ways do you use the Scriptures?

(17:16-21) To whom does Paul make his first appeal? Why might he have begun there? How is Athenian life characterized in verse 21? Are there ways that this description can apply to your life? Explain.

(17:16, 22-31) What can you conclude about the type of worship practiced by the Athenians? How does Paul use their religious practices as an open door to share his faith? What arguments does Paul make against the worship of idols?

What idea, verse, or phrase from this chapter can change your experience today?

Day 107
Acts 18

Background: Paul remained in Corinth as a tentmaker (verse 3). Even today the practice of tentmaking continues. Preachers who serve churches or are in ministries with limited financial resources often earn a portion of their income by working in another field.

(18:1-8) What important role do people like Aquila and Priscilla (verses 2-3), Jason (17:5-7), and Lydia (16:15) play in the spread of the gospel? How have you used your personal resources to further the spread of God's word?

(18:9-11) What encouragement does Paul receive from the Lord? How does he respond? What encouragement have you received from God? How have you responded?

(18:18-26) What practice does Paul demonstrate with Priscilla and Aquila as he did with Timothy (16:3)? Who do Aquila and Priscilla in turn spend time instructing? Who has been your spiritual mentor? Who are you mentoring now?

(18:27-28) How does the Corinthian church treat Apollos when he expresses a desire to go to the region of Achaia? What is the result of his visit there? What lesson can churches today learn from the examples in this chapter?

What idea, verse, or phrase from this chapter can change your experience today?

Day 108
Acts 19

Background: This chapter seems to support the practice of "rebaptism." Paul, though, makes a clear distinction between John the baptizer's baptism of repentance and Jesus' baptism in the Spirit. Those today who suggest that a person should be baptized again deny what God has done in that first baptism.

(19:1-10) How does Paul deal with the resistance encountered in the synagogue? What was the result of this adjustment? What does this teach you about the importance of persistence in sharing God's message?

(19:11-20) What happens when Jesus' name is used with respect? What happens when it is not? When is the name of Jesus misused today? When is it mistreated? What can you do to make sure that the name of Jesus is held in high honor?

(19:23-27) Why are the silversmiths upset with Paul? What is at risk for them? In what ways today do religious teachings come in conflict with the pursuit of profit? When does God object to the making of money? How are you striving to keep God ahead of materialism?

(19:35-41) What wisdom does the town clerk show in his words to the crowd?

What idea, verse, or phrase from this chapter can change your experience today?

Day 109
Acts 20

Background: Many different places are named in Acts as Paul and his colleagues strive to spread the word of God. Most of these are within the boundaries of the Roman Empire and its worship of many gods. The book of Acts is the triumph of the Christian church to carry the gospel of Jesus throughout the world in spite of severe persecution.

(20:1-6) Why does Paul retrace his steps and return to many cities he had already visited? Note how many different people from different cities Paul now has traveling and studying with him. Why would Paul recruit so many people from so many different places?

(20:7-12) What causes the death of Eutychus? (Apparently Paul was not always the most interesting preacher!) How does God turn this unfortunate event into a positive one for the church at Troas?

(20:7, 11) What common practice is mentioned here? (The "breaking of bread" probably refers to the celebration of the Lord's Supper.) On what day of the week does this take place? The Sabbath is the last day of the week. Why would the church celebrate the Lord's Supper on the first day of the week (see Luke 24:1-8)?

(20:18-35) What does Paul say is the most crucial work in his life? How has he kept it most important? What is the most significant thing in your life? What are you doing to keep it central?

What idea, verse, or phrase from this chapter can change your experience today?

Day 110
Acts 21

Background: One of the things that actually gives credibility to Luke's history in Acts is his recording of the failures of the early Christian church as well as its successes. Sometimes the church was fiercely united, as when it prayed for Peter's release (chapter 12). Sometimes, though, it was divided, as when Paul and Barnabas argued (chapter 15) and here.

(21:1-6) Does Paul seem to suddenly be ignoring the direction of the Spirit? Explain. Why might the instructions of the Spirit to one person seem to be in conflict with the instructions to another? How is this conflict resolved?

(21:10-14) Why do the Christians beg Paul not to go to Jerusalem? Why does Paul say he must? Why do you think they said, "The Lord's will be done" (verse 14)?

(21:17-26) What is the Christians' concern with regard to Paul? Why do they have this concern? What does Paul do? Read 1 Corinthians 9:19-23. What is Paul's primary focus in everything that he does?

(21:37-40) What does Paul do even in the midst of his arrest? What opportunity is he given? What would have happened if Paul had listened to his Christian friends in verses 4 and 12? Did his decision agree with the direction of the Spirit as he understood it? Explain.

What idea, verse, or phrase from this chapter can change your experience today?

Day 111
Acts 22

Background: One of the characteristics of Luke's writing is the skillful presentation of dramatic speeches. In this speech, Paul recounts his own conversion from Acts 9. His narrative is filled with quotations and visual descriptions.

(22:1-5) Why does Paul share this information with the crowd (see Acts 21:27-28)? In what ways is he identifying with the crowd? How might this background help his presentation of the gospel?

(22:6-21) What does Paul say was God's plan for him? Why does Paul say he had to tell preach and teach in the synagogues and elsewhere? What confession does Paul make? Where will you tell others about Jesus? How much risk are you willing to take to share this message? Who will you tell today?

(22:22) How does the crowd respond to Paul's story? Why do they react this way? Why might the good news of Jesus be received with resistance today?

(22:23-29) What defense does Paul use with his Roman captors? Again, how does Paul become "all things to all people" (1 Corinthians 9:22)? How does it help Paul in this situation? How could it help him to share the gospel? Which of your qualities or experiences can help you to become all things to all people?

What idea, verse, or phrase from this chapter can change your experience today?

Day 112
Acts 23

Background: The Sanhedrin was the supreme court for the Jews. In New Testament times, the Sanhedrin was made up of the chief priests, the temple elders, and teachers of the law. Paul's response in verse 5 may be explained by his poor eyesight (see Galatians 4:15 and 6:11), or that he was suggesting that the high priest would not behave this way, or that he refused to accept Ananias as high priest.

(22:30-23:10) What differences are there between the beliefs of the Pharisees and those of the Sadducees? How does Paul use these differences to his own advantage? How are you becoming more aware of the beliefs of those to whom God is sending you to witness?

(23:11) How does the Lord encourage Paul? What warning or prophecy is given to Paul? When has God encouraged you in a meaningful way? How did it help you?

(23:12-15) What do the Jews who oppose Paul's plan decide to do? Can you think of any circumstances when those who follow God would have to resort to violence? Explain.

(23:16-35) How is Paul now saved from death? Do you think God is involved in this intervention? Why or why not? What opportunity might this now give Paul? Pay attention to the opportunities God gives you to witness today!

What idea, verse, or phrase from this chapter can change your experience today?

Day 113
Acts 24

Background: Another of Luke's purposes in writing this book was to show that Christians were not enemies of the Roman government. Even though many of the early Christians were arrested, tried, and even put to death, the Christians were always orderly and peaceful in their presentation of the gospel message.

(24:1-9) How do the Jews seek to win the favor of Governor Felix? What charges do they bring against Paul? How have their accusations changed (compare verse 6 with 21:28)? What does this suggest about the truth of their charges?

(24:10-16) How does Paul answer the charges against him? Note that Paul makes sure to include a witness for the Christian faith. What does he say about "the Way" that might appeal to the Romans? What does he say that might make Christianity appeal to the Jews present?

(24:17-21) Why does Paul point out the fact that the Asian Jews are not present? What does their absence suggest about their charges against Paul?

(24:22-26) What kind of a person does Felix seem to be? What topics does Paul cover in his conversations with Felix? Why might these topics cause Felix to be afraid?

What idea, verse, or phrase from this chapter can change your experience today?

Day 114
Acts 25

Background: In 59-60 A.D., Felix was recalled to Rome to answer charges about disturbances and questionable conduct in his rule of Judea. His desire to grant a favor to the Jews (24:27) was to appease those he would be facing at trial in Rome. The record of Festus's rule shows him to be a man of wisdom and honesty.

(25:1-5) What emotions might motivate the Jews to persist in their desire to have Paul killed? What might their continued efforts to commit murder suggest about their own awareness of the truth of their charges against Paul?

(25:6-8) What remains consistent about Paul's defense? In what three areas does Paul defend himself? Can Paul honor the practices of the Jews and the laws of Rome and still keep Jesus first? Explain. How does putting God first direct you to have respect for the practices of others and the laws of the government?

(25:9-12) What risk would Paul take by going to Jerusalem for trial? What opportunity would he have if his case were heard in Rome? What would it mean for the Christian faith if the emperor of Rome found Paul innocent of the charges that would stop his witness for Jesus?

(25:23-27) What is Festus hoping that Agrippa will help him do? What does it suggest that even though Festus can find no guilt in Paul, he continues to hold him?

What idea, verse, or phrase from this chapter can change your experience today?

Day 115
Acts 26

Background: Once again, Paul sets an example for us all. Every situation for Paul becomes an opportunity to witness for Jesus. Not even the threat of death can turn Paul away from the mission to which God has called him. That mission belongs to all of us!

(26:1-3) What qualities does Paul commend in King Agrippa? Why is it important that he has Agrippa evaluating his case from this point of reference?

(26:4-11) To which promise of God does Paul refer? Again Paul speaks about how greatly he opposed Jesus before he tells how Jesus chose him. How does this help his witness? How far were you from Jesus before Jesus chose you?

(26:12-18) To whom did Jesus say Paul would be sent to witness? What things did Jesus specifically say Paul's witness would accomplish? What can your witness for Jesus do in the lives of others? Ask Jesus to help you do these things for him.

(26:19-31) What things impress you most about Paul's final appeal in his presentation? About what does he seem to be most passionate? How would you feel if someone spoke Paul's words in verse 29 to you? Keep these feelings in mind as you offer your witness and prayers to others who do not know the Lord.

What idea, verse, or phrase from this chapter can change your experience today?

Day 116
Acts 27

Background: Once again, the record of Acts is presented from a "we" perspective. While it is very likely that Luke was nearby during Paul's imprisonment in Caesarea, he now rejoins him as Paul sails to Rome. Though Luke may have in mind keeping a first-hand account of the events of Paul's life, it is more likely that his desire is to support Paul in whatever way he can.

(27:1-44) Give a summary of the main events of this chapter. Describe Julius, the centurion in charge of this trip. How does Paul's role change in the course of this journey?

(27:21-26) What message of hope does Paul receive from God? How does Paul use this message as an opportunity to witness to his fellow travelers? How has God comforted and encouraged you in times of trial? When have you used God's words to comfort others in their time of trouble? Have you ever done this for someone who was not a Christian? If so, when?

(27:33-38) How can Paul show this level of compassion for his captors? How does he continue to share the message of God with those on the ship? Do you pray openly in front of strangers before eating? Why or why not? In what other public situations could you pray even if those present may not be believers?

What idea, verse, or phrase from this chapter can change your experience today?

Day 117
Acts 28

Background: The book of Acts ends without telling us what happens to Paul. Details in some of Paul's letters suggest that he was able to return to visit some of the churches in Asia Minor, Crete, and Greece. Tradition holds that Paul even went to Spain to witness for Jesus. Paul finally returned to Rome in 67 A.D. and was martyred in 67 or 68.

(28:1-10) What does Paul do during this stay in Malta? Do you look for opportunities to serve others, even strangers? Why or why not? What miracles does God perform through Paul? What do you suspect Paul did following each of these events?

(28:11-16) Who does Paul encounter in Puteoli, the Forum of Appius, and the Three Taverns? How do these meetings affect Paul? Do you seek out the company of other believers when you travel? How do these encounters affect you?

(28:17-28) What does Paul try to do now? What opportunity does this provide for him? What are the results of his witnessing? Why do you think Paul again uses words that might anger his Jewish listeners?

(28:30-31) Though under house arrest for two years, what does Paul seek to do? How does verse 31 suggest God assisted Paul? What circumstances keep you from witnessing for Jesus? How can you change that today?

What idea, verse, or phrase from this chapter can change your experience today?

Day 118
Romans 1

Background: The apostle Paul wrote the Letter to the Romans to the people of the Christian church in Rome. It is the best organized of Paul's letters, focusing on the central message of the good news of Jesus Christ and God's plan for the salvation of humankind.

(1:1-7) How does Paul describe himself? What does Paul say about the gospel? What does Paul tell his readers about Jesus? How does Paul describe his readers? How does this description fit you?

(1:8-15) Why does Paul give thanks for the church in Rome? What does Paul do for them? Why does Paul hope to visit this church? For whom do you give thanks in Christ? Why? What mutual encouragement do you share with that person?

(1:16-17) In your own words, what is the message of this passage?

(1:18-20) What does Paul say that people have failed to recognize? Why have they done this? What does Paul warn will come to these people?

(1:21-32) With what words and phrases does Paul describe humankind? Could Paul's descriptions fit today's society? Explain.

What idea, verse, or phrase from this chapter can change your experience today?

Day 119
Romans 2

Background: In verses 6-7 and 10, Paul seems to suggest to the Jews that according to their doctrine, good works will assure a person of eternal life. In the next chapter, though, Paul says that all people are justified by God's grace, not by works of the law. This is consistent with the rest of Paul's teachings.

(2:1-4) How does Paul's teaching here agree with that of Jesus in Matthew 7:1? On what basis does God judge? Why might a Christian be jealous of God's kindness shown to another? Why should he or she not be jealous? Be aware of the times when you judge others today.

(2:8-11) What will come to those who reject God's truth? How does Amos 3:1-2 help you to understand Paul saying Jews first and then Gentiles? Does God show any partiality in judgment? Explain.

(2:17-24) Why does Paul understand so well the thinking of the Jews (see Acts 22:3)? Who are those that the Jews would consider "the blind," "in the dark," "the foolish," and "infants"? Of what are the Jews guilty when they think of others in this way?

(2:25-29) Circumcision was a sign of the covenant God made with Israel (see Genesis 17:2, 9-10). What error does Paul point out in Jewish thinking? What does Paul mean by "circumcision of the heart"? From where does this "circumcision" originate?

What idea, verse, or phrase from this chapter can change your experience today?

Day 120
Romans 3

Background: One of Paul's concerns in writing to the Roman church was that the Gentile Christians were treating the Jewish Christians like outcasts. The reason for this rejection was the practice of the Jewish Christians to observe certain dietary rules and holy days.

(3:1-8) What responsibility do you think comes with being entrusted with the words of God (verse 2)? How does the unrighteousness of a person bring out the righteousness of God more clearly?

(3:9-18) What does Paul say all people have in common? What happens to those who turn away from God?

(3:19-20) Is it possible for anyone to completely keep the law of God? Explain. What then will be the result of trying to earn God's favor by keeping the law? What is the purpose of the law?

(3:21-26) How does true righteousness come? What does Paul say here that all people have in common? How does deliverance from slavery to sin (redemption) come? Who is it that God justifies?

(3:27-31) What is the sole basis for being able to boast? How is a person justified? If we are made right with God through our faith alone, why then does a believer try to keep the law?

What idea, verse, or phrase from this chapter can change your experience today?

Day 121
Romans 4

Background: Abraham is the great patriarch or forefather of the Jewish nation. God made a promise to Abraham that Jews would be the source of a blessing to the entire world. That blessing became reality in Jesus, although, ironically, the Jews did not recognize him in that way.

(4:1-3) On what basis do the Jews seem to think that Abraham earned God's favor (verse 2)? Why would that be a reason for boasting? What does Scripture say is the real reason that God found Abraham righteous? On what basis will God find you righteous today?

(4:4-8) Explain the difference between works and faith. How do works seek to control God? Why are the blessings received in faith a gift rather than a wage? According to David, what blessings are received from God when one lives in faith rather than works?

(4:9-17) What does Paul say were not the ways that Abraham received God's blessings? What was the only basis for the blessings Abraham received from God? For what two reasons can Abraham be claimed as forefather? Which of these is the reason you claim Abraham as father?

(4:18-25) What was it that seemed impossible for Abraham? Why would Abraham continue to hope that this would happen? What has God done in your life that you would have considered impossible? What is to be the focus of our faith?

What idea, verse, or phrase from this chapter can change your experience today?

Day 122
Romans 5

Background: The Letter to the Romans is a well-crafted explanation of how we, though sinful, can be found righteous before God. Paul repeatedly stresses that faith alone in Jesus is the only way we can be found acceptable by God.

(5:1-8) How does Jesus give us access to God? What is the peace that this relationship with God brings? Why should we rejoice in suffering? When has suffering increased your hope and faith?

(5:9-11) Why would Paul call us "God's enemies"? What changes that relationship? Verse 10 suggests that our salvation is an ongoing blessing. What does this ongoing blessing mean for you?

(5:12-14, 18-19) What contrasts does Paul make between Adam and Jesus? How can the death that comes through sin be understood as both physical and spiritual death? How can the life that Christ brings be understood both physically and spiritually? Describe the life you have found in Christ Jesus.

(5:20-21) How does the law (like the Ten Commandments) make us more aware of our sinfulness? Why would the increase of sin result in the increase of grace?

What idea, verse, or phrase from this chapter can change your experience today?

Day 123
Romans 6

Background: The concept that salvation comes through faith alone (3:23-24, 28) is sometimes called "cheap grace." This is because it may be thought that one can do whatever one wishes so long as one believes. Yet this grace is not cheap but costly, because it cost Jesus his life.

(6:1-4) If grace increases as sin increases (5:20), should we then continue trying to sin? Why or why not? Through what event do we die to sin? How does this happen? What do we receive as a result of this event?

(6:3-11) Describe the ways that baptism connects us to Jesus. Once we are united with Jesus, how does our relationship to sin change? What then is the focus of our lives? How have you made this the focus for your life?

(6:11-14) Paul here gives us a guide for the Christian's victory over sin. Identify each step:

Step 1 (verse 11)

Step 2 (verse 12)

Step 3 (verse 13)

(6:15-23) Describe life under sin. Describe life under righteousness. What is the result of a life enslaved to sin? What is the result of a life enslaved to God's righteousness?

What idea, verse, or phrase from this chapter can change your experience today?

Day 124
Romans 7

Background: In this chapter, Paul gives a wonderful description of the struggle with sin that all Christians face. Even though we wish to live the life that God desires for us, we cannot help but choose to sin. This does not excuse our sins, but rather points again to our need for the grace of Christ.

(7:1-6) How long does the law have authority over a person? How do we die to the law (see 6:4)? How does the law stimulate sin within us? For what does death to the law free us?

(7:7-13) How does the law make us aware of our sins? How does the law bring death? Is Paul saying that the law is good or not? Explain.

(7:14-20) Explain the contradiction Paul presents in verses 15 and 19. Have you ever felt this frustration? If so, when? Ask God to help you through this kind of difficulty whenever it presents itself.

(7:21-25) What are the two laws about which Paul is speaking? Where does he find these two laws at work? To which of these laws is Paul a slave? To which of these laws are you a slave? How can this be? What answer does Paul give for his question in verse 24? Who will rescue you from your body of sin?

What idea, verse, or phrase from this chapter can change your experience today?

Day 125
Romans 8

Background: Paul uses the word law in several different ways in his Letter to the Romans. In 2:17-20, 9:31, and 10:3-5, it refers to God's law. In 3:21, Paul is referring to the Ten Commandments, while in 3:19, he is talking about the entire Old Testament. In 3:27, Paul uses law to mean a principle or rule, and in this chapter he uses it to mean a controlling power or force.

(8:1-4) What did God do that the law could not? How did God accomplish this? What requirement was met by this act of God (see 6:23)?

(8:5-8) Contrast the life of sin with life in the Spirit.

(8:12-17) Look at Paul's description of life in the Spirit. What responsibilities are named? What promises? What privileges? What things show that you are living in the Spirit?

(8:18-27) What is our future hope (verses 22-23)? What does this hope promise to us (verse 24)? How does the Holy Spirit help us?

(8:31-39) What are the three reasons Paul says we cannot be condemned (verse 34)? Over what things does Paul say we are conquerors? How is it that we have this victory?

What idea, verse, or phrase from this chapter can change your experience today?

Day 126
Romans 9

Background: Originally, the "people of Israel" referred to the descendants of Jacob, who received the new name Israel by God. From the time of the exodus, it was used for the entire nation. Later, when the nation divided, it referred to the northern kingdom. The southern kingdom was called Judah. In New Testament times, it meant the chosen people of God. Paul is saying here that despite Israel's disobedience, God has stayed faithful to God's promises.

(9:1-5) Describe the connection between the conscience and the Holy Spirit. What does this suggest to you about the expression "guilty conscience"? What two things does Paul say about the nature of Jesus Christ in verse 5?

(9:14-18) The previous section spoke of God's apparent failure to bestow grace upon Israel because of their rejection of Jesus. How does Paul respond to this? What weight do our desires or efforts carry with God?

(9:19-21) Have we any grounds to question God? Explain. Toward what purpose has God shaped you? Are you striving to fulfill God's purpose? If so, how?

(9:30-33) On what grounds did the Gentiles seek God's mercy? Through what means did the Jews seek it? Which method are you using?

What idea, verse, or phrase from this chapter can change your experience today?

Day 127
Romans 10

Background: In many of his letters, Paul prays for the churches to which he wrote (Ephesians 1:15-23; Colossians 1:3; 1 Thessalonians 1:2-3; 2 Thessalonians 1:3). Here he prays that his fellow Israelites might receive God's salvation.

(10:1-4) What errors did the people of Israel make in their pursuit of God's righteousness? What truth does Paul pray that they might know?

(10:5-7) How does living by the law (by works) seek to control Christ? What is the flaw in that way of living?

(10:8-11) What is the relationship between confession and belief? What does this suggest about the importance of witness to others about Christ? What assurance does Scripture give for those who risk on Christ's behalf? How are you witnessing to your faith?

(10:12-13) How can Jews be saved? How can Gentiles be saved?

(10:14-15) Paul states in reverse order the four necessary steps to be able to call on Christ. What are they in proper order? What things are you doing that will allow God to call your feet "beautiful"?

What idea, verse, or phrase from this chapter can change your experience today?

Day 128
Romans 11

Background: One of the difficult issues that comes up is that of God's plan for the Jews. Since they do not believe that Jesus is the Savior, will they be saved? Certainly they were and are God's first chosen people. And ultimately it is not a question for us—it is God's decision. Our task as Christians is to share Jesus with anyone we can.

(11:1-10) What does Paul say about God's feelings toward the remnant of Israel? What is the basis for God's choice? What does Paul say about works and grace?

(11:11-16) Read verses 12 and 15 together. Summarize their message. Who does Paul say he was called to bring to Christ? Who would you like to bring to Christ? Decide how you will try to do this.

(11:17-24) Why should the believer not be arrogant or boastful? What does Paul teach about the nature of God? When in your life have you felt God's sternness? When have you felt God's kindness?

(11:25-32) What is Paul's understanding of God's final decision regarding the Jews? Does that seem fair? Explain. Look at the parable in Matthew 20:1-16. How do you understand God's plans for Israel in light of this parable? Why can we now rejoice? Take a few moments to thank God for God's great mercy.

What idea, verse, or phrase from this chapter can change your experience today?

Day 129
Romans 12

Background: The term *grace* can be understood through the acronym, "God's Riches At Christ's Expense." The blessings of God are available to us only because Jesus gave his life for us on the cross. Whatever we as Christians do is the way we thank God for this great sacrifice.

(12:1-2) What kind of behavior does Paul encourage us to follow? What are some specific ways that we might do this? How is this behavior an act of worship? Why should we do this?

(12:3-5) What part of the human body are you most like? Why? What are the strengths and abilities of this body part? In what ways does it depend upon the other parts of the body? How do you support the other members of the body of Christ? How do you look to them for support?

(12:6-8) What gifts or abilities has God given you? How are you using these gifts for the body of Christ? How do you feel when you are using your gifts for the glory of God?

(12:9-21) How do all these instructions reflect the nature of Christian love? Which of these is easiest for you to follow? Why? Which is most difficult? Again, why? Choose one you will spend this week trying to develop as part of your Christian walk.

What idea, verse, or phrase from this chapter can change your experience today?

Day 130
Romans 13

Background: A wealthy young man believed that Christianity was right and true, but could not turn away from his sin. One day he was reading this chapter of Romans, particularly verse 14, and became a Christian. This young man was Augustine, later the Bishop of Hippo and one of the most influential Christians in the past 2,000 years.

(13:1-2) Who do Christians believe to be the only authority in their lives? Why then should Christians obey the government and its rules? Does it matter whether those in authority are Christian? Explain. Can you think of a time when Christians should not follow the laws of the government?

(13:3-5) What two motivations does Paul give for obeying the authority of the government? Which of these is your primary reason for obeying the laws of our society? What does that suggest to you about your walk with God?

(13:6-7) Do Paul's words here agree with those of Jesus in Matthew 22:15-22? Explain. What responsibility does this suggest to those who are in positions of authority?

(13:8-10) How does love for others fulfill the law? How does the "debt of love" always remain "outstanding"? In what special way will you "love your neighbor" today?

What idea, verse, or phrase from this chapter can change your experience today?

Day 131
Romans 14

Background: There is a danger for mature Christians to judge the practices of immature Christians and for those new to the faith to criticize the practices of those with more experience. Apparently, this was a significant problem in Rome. As you reflect on Paul's words here, consider how well they match the teachings of Jesus.

(14:1-6) Summarize Paul's words in this section. Does one's diet have any significance for salvation? Explain. What matters for salvation? What are some examples of religious practices that have created divisions between Christians?

(14:7-8) Who stands with us in life? In death? How does life in Jesus bind us to other Christians?

(14:9-12) How is it that Jesus is Lord of both the living and the dead? On what basis can we make judgments of the religious practices of others? What is the danger in doing this (see Matthew 7:1-5)?

(14:19-23) What are the most important considerations when we make choices in our public behavior? Why is it important for the faith of other Christians to keep your thoughts about their practices between you and God? Of what benefit would this be to you? What will you do this week to fulfill Paul's challenge in verse 19?

What idea, verse, or phrase from this chapter can change your experience today?

Day 132
Romans 15

Background: Some ancient handwritten copies of this letter have the closing (16:25-27) at the end of chapter 14. As you read the last two chapters of Romans, consider why these copies, circulated to other Christian churches, might have left off these chapters.

(15:1-3) What would be accomplished by seeking to please our Christian neighbor? What should motivate us to act in this fashion? Who did Christ seek to please by his sacrifice on the cross?

(15:4-13) What is the purpose of Scripture? What things does this passage say God gives to us? What does Paul repeatedly name as the primary purpose for these gifts and for everything we do? How are you seeking to fulfill this purpose?

(15:14-22) How does Paul seek to build up the Roman church? Does it seem that Paul is boasting in this passage? Explain. What things does Paul say he has been able to do through Christ? What is the offering Paul seeks to bring to God? What offering will you try to give to God?

(15:23-33) Why does Paul believe he has no further ministry in his current location (see verse 20)? What example of social ministry is mentioned here? How is your congregation involved in social ministry? What specifically are you doing to assist the poor in other places?

What idea, verse, or phrase from this chapter can change your experience today?

Day 133
Romans 16

Background: Scholars have questioned how Paul could have known so many people in a church he had never visited. Yet many of us have friends who have moved to other cities. Another consideration is that Paul had heard of these individuals and greeted them as brothers and sisters in Christ, commending them for their partnership in the gospel.

(16:1-15, 21-23) Read this list carefully. What do you learn about Paul as you read these many greetings? What does this list teach you about the Christian church, both then and now?

(16:3-4) What do we know about Priscilla and Aquila (see Acts 18:2-3, 18-19)? What more does Paul tells us about them here?

(16:16) What practice(s) in your congregation might be compared with a "holy kiss" greeting? How does your congregation send greeting and encouragement to other churches?

(16:17-20) What warnings are given here? Are these warnings applicable today? Explain.

(16:25-27) What is it that this passage says God can do? What is the ultimate purpose of all things (see also 15:5-9)?

What idea, verse, or phrase from this chapter can change your experience today?

Day 134
1 Corinthians 1

Background: Sosthenes, from whom Paul also sends greetings, may have been the synagogue ruler at Corinth (see Acts 18:17-18). Obviously Sosthenes became a Christian, possibly through the influence of Paul, or of Apollos who also ministered in Corinth (see Acts 19:1).

(1:1-9) To whom is this church dedicated? Why does Paul give thanks for these people? What blessings have they received through faith? What promise do they have?

(1:10-17) What problem do the Corinthians seem to have within their church? What is it that divides them? What does Paul say that should unite them in mind and thought?

(1:18-25) What makes the cross foolishness to the world? What makes it power to the Christian? How is the cross a stumbling block to the Jews who looked for a triumphant, political savior? How is it foolishness to the Gentiles who had no respect for a criminal?

(1:26-31) Of what could the Corinthian church members boast before coming to faith in Christ? Of what could you boast before your faith in Christ became real? Why, in the eyes of the world, is God's choice of the Corinthians (and you) foolish? How is it wisdom? On what occasions are you able to boast in the Lord?

What idea, verse, or phrase from this chapter can change your experience today?

Day 135
1 Corinthians 2

Background: The city of Corinth was one of the chief cities—if not the chief city—of Greece in Paul's day. It is estimated that Corinth had a population of 250,000 free persons and 400,000 slaves. It was a crossroads for travelers and traders. Paul visited Corinth during his third missionary trip of 53-57 A.D.

(2:1-5) With what attitude did Paul witness to the Corinthians? What does Paul recall to support this claim? What did Paul seek to make the sole focus of his time with the Corinthians? In what ways do you seek to make this your primary focus in your relationships with others?

(2:6) Are the "mature" of whom Paul is speaking those Christians who are deeply rooted in the faith? Do you consider yourself to be a mature Christian? Explain. What are you doing to become or remain a mature Christian?

(2:6-10a) What demonstrates that the rulers of Paul's day did not understand God's wisdom? What is the wisdom that the world today offers? How is that wisdom coming to nothing? How is Christ being "crucified" today?

(2:10b-16) From where does the wisdom of God come? What does the spiritual person receive from God?

What idea, verse, or phrase from this chapter can change your experience today?

Day 136
1 Corinthians 3

Background: Paul had heard from several sources that the Corinthian church was experiencing division. One reason for this division was competition based on who had been baptized by whom (see 1:13-17). This rivalry revealed the spiritual immaturity of the members.

(3:1-3) How does Paul describe the Corinthians? What behavior on the part of the Corinthians supports his description?

(3:4-9) What made the Corinthians' argument empty? What should have been the source of their boasting? What roles did Paul and Apollos play in the Corinthian church? What was the true reason for this congregation's growth? Who has done the planting and tilling in your congregation? In what ways has God made your church grow?

(3:10-15) What is the true foundation of any church? In what ways does your congregation reveal its true foundation? What are you doing to help build on this foundation a structure that will withstand divine judgment?

(3:16-17) How are you making your body the kind of place where God would wish to dwell?

What idea, verse, or phrase from this chapter can change your experience today?

Day 137
1 Corinthians 4

Background: Much of what Paul strives to communicate to the Corinthians is that the message of Christ crucified and risen is far more important than the messenger who brings it. When anyone (including us) seeks to win personal glory, then the glory of God is diminished.

(4:1-5) To whom does Paul consider himself accountable? What freedom does that give him? What words does Paul use to suggest that sharing the gospel is an act of stewardship? How have you been a good steward of the good news of God's love and forgiveness?

(4:6-7) What does Paul name as one of the causes of division? Summarize why Paul says we have no reason for boasting.

(4:8-13) What is the wealth that the Corinthians have received? Describe Paul's current situation. How, in this predicament, can Paul still show this concern for the Corinthians?

(4:14-17) How does Paul feel about the Corinthians? In what way is he like a father to them? How does he show his concern for them?

What idea, verse, or phrase from this chapter can change your experience today?

Day 138
1 Corinthians 5

Background: In addition to divisions, the Corinthian church was also struggling with immoral practices. A large city like this had many temples and was a center for many forms of pagan immorality. It is no surprise that a church in this culture could struggle so.

(5:1-2) For what had the Corinthians previously been bragging (see 1:11-15, 3:4)? Why does Paul say they should feel no pride? Is he speaking to individuals or to the entire church? Why? Does Paul's instruction for this sin seem harsh for today's world? Explain.

(5:3-5) By whose name and power does Paul pass judgment on the "immoral" Corinthian man? Of what value would it be to the church to expel this man from the church? Of what value might it be to the man? What is the danger in judging sin? What is the danger in ignoring it? Who in the church should pass these judgments? On what basis?

(5:6-8) What "yeast" does Paul warn against? What "yeast" does he encourage? What yeast in your life is working against your relationship with God? What will you do today to get rid of it?

(5:9-13) How might others perceive our associations with the immoral in our congregations? Why, at the same time, do we need to be "in the world, but not of the world"?

What idea, verse, or phrase from this chapter can change your experience today?

Day 139
1 Corinthians 6

Background: Much of this letter is concerned with the behavior of Christians toward the other members of the body of Christ. Repeatedly, this congregation has failed to treat one another with Christian love, choosing instead to follow worldly practices.

(6:1-6) What instruction is given about the resolution of disputes among the believers? What example does their current practices set for non-Christians? Why would it be better for them to judge their disputes among themselves? How are disputes handled in your congregation?

(6:7-8) How have the Corinthian Christians lost their way? What have they made most important? Why would it be better for them to be wronged, even if it was by another member of the church?

(6:9-11) Do you think Paul is saying that a Christian could never commit any of these sins? Explain. Is Paul saying that those who commit these sins can never enter the kingdom of God? Explain. How do these sinful acts push one out of the kingdom? How does repetition of these acts keep one outside the kingdom?

(6:12-20) How does life in Christ allow us to do whatever we wish? From a spiritual perspective, why would it not always be good for us to do whatever we wish? Why is sexual immorality so dangerous for members of the church?

What idea, verse, or phrase from this chapter can change your experience today?

Day 140
1 Corinthians 7

Background: Paul's answer to the Corinthians regarding marriage suggests that all of us should avoid marriage unless we simply cannot control ourselves. Paul, though, believed that Jesus would return during his lifetime, and intimate relationships between the sexes, even in marriage, would open the door for dangerous temptations.

(7:1-5) What instructions does Paul give for the marriage relationship? How can such practices help encourage husbands and wives in their Christian walk?

(7:12-14) What instruction is given to those Christians who are married to non-Christians? How might staying together in this case be a blessing to the marriage and to the family? If the unbelieving spouse leaves, is the Christian spouse free to remarry (see 7:11)?

(7:17-24) What makes it difficult to be contented in the circumstances into which God has placed a person? What knowledge can make a person's circumstances joyful? What joy do you find in your life's situation?

(7:32-35) Do you agree with Paul's assessment that the attention of married people will be in this world and not with God? Why or why not? What are some things that wives and husbands can do to help themselves and each other to be focused on matters of faith?

What idea, verse, or phrase from this chapter can change your experience today?

Day 141
1 Corinthians 8

Background: It was the practice in Corinth to offer meat and other food on pagan altars. That which was left over from the sacrifice might be eaten by the priests, by the family making the offering and their friends, or sold in the market. The Corinth Christians argued whether this eating made their witness to Christ less genuine.

(8:1-3) Contrast knowledge with love. What should be the source of this love? Do you base your decisions more on knowledge or on Christian love? Explain.

(8:4-6) Of what important Christian principle does Paul remind his readers? How does this principle inform one who struggles with the decision about eating food sacrificed to idols? If an idol is nothing at all, what happens to the food sacrificed to it?

(8:7-8) Why might eating food sacrificed to idols cause some Christians to feel guilty? What is the Christian principle that Paul offers here?

(8:9-13) What freedom does the Christian find in Christ? What warning does Paul give to the mature Christian? What practices might a Christian today want to avoid so as not to cause another believer to sin? Comment on this teaching in relation to Paul's first comments about knowledge and love (8:1-3).

What idea, verse, or phrase from this chapter can change your experience today?

Day 142
1 Corinthians 9

Background: Part of the genius of Paul's letters is his ability to take a real, practical problem and provide real, practical answers. On the way to these answers, though, Paul reveals some of the principles of true Christian living.

(9:1-2) What two things does Paul list to prove his apostleship?

(9:3-14) What criticism does Paul seem to have received from some of the Corinthians? What examples does Paul list of other workers who receive compensation for their work? What does this suggest to you about a pastor's salary?

(9:12, 15) For what support did Paul ask the Corinthians? Why did he do this?

(9:15-23) Why is Paul not able to boast in his ministry of the gospel? How does this make him like a slave? To what ministry has God called you? In what ways have you become all things to all people to further your ministry?

(9:24-27) What "training" do you follow to keep yourself in shape for the ministry to which God has called you? How do these practices keep you from being "disqualified" from the prize that God offers?

What idea, verse, or phrase from this chapter can change your experience today?

Day 143
1 Corinthians 10

Background: Paul now broadens the focus of the topic. Rather than just food offered to idols, Paul now makes it an issue of considering oneself too strong in the faith to be concerned about such "trivial" things.

(10:1-10) What blessings had the Israelites of the exodus received from God? How did the Israelites respond to these blessings (see Exodus 16:1-3; 17:1-3; Numbers 14:1-4)? For whom were the Israelites concerned? How is this like the Corinthians? How is this like some Christians today?

(10:11-13) What is the warning for the Corinthians and for us? What promise do you find in verse 13? What situation in your life can this promise help you face today?

(10:14-22) How would participating in pagan practices make the Lord jealous? How does the body and blood of Christ unite us with all Christians? What does that suggest to you about our relationship with other Christian groups today? How is your congregation working with other Christians?

(10:31-33) What should guide all our decisions? What should we always seek to avoid? For what reason do we strive to do these things?

What idea, verse, or phrase from this chapter can change your experience today?

Day 144
1 Corinthians 11

Background: The next section of the letter was designed to put the matters at hand to rest. However it has triggered much argument in the Christian church. It should be remembered that Paul was writing about a specific situation in Corinth. While the specifics may not apply today, the broader principles will always apply.

(11:1) Who is the ultimate example? Who is it that follows that example? Whose example are we to follow? Explain the logic of this order.

(11:3) What does Paul say is the order of honor or authority? Comment on this in light of the order of creation.

(11:4-10) In Paul's day, men worshiped with their heads uncovered and women with their heads covered. Ignoring this practice would dishonor what "head"? What is the larger lesson being taught here about worship practices?

(11:17-22) What is the practice of these Christians at their potluck dinners (agape or "love" feast) held in conjunction with the Lord's Supper? The divisions in Corinth were likely between the rich and the poor. Between whom do divisions exist today in the church?

(11:27-32) What does communion mean for you?

What idea, verse, or phrase from this chapter can change your experience today?

Day 145
1 Corinthians 12

Background: Yet another source of division in the Corinthian congregation was over the issue of spiritual gifts. We actually can be thankful for this controversy, because the result is a passage that is one of the best loved by and most wonderfully descriptive of the church—the body of Christ.

(12:3-6) What four things have their source in the Spirit of God?

(12:7-11, 27-30) What gifts are listed here? What is the purpose of spiritual gifts? On what basis does a person have specific gifts?

(12:12-20) Describe the relationship between the members of the church based on this description of the parts of the body. What part of the body might best describe your role in the church? Why?

(12:21-25) What responsibilities do the parts of the body share? What happens if the body of Christ suffers from division? How do the various "parts of the body" help one another in your congregation?

(12:26) When has your congregation suffered together when one member has suffered? When has your congregation received honor for the contribution of one member or part?

What idea, verse, or phrase from this chapter can change your experience today?

Day 146
1 Corinthians 13

Background: Paul now turns to the one spiritual gift without which all the other gifts are nothing. This passage on love is often appropriately read at weddings. However, couples should realize that it does not speak of romantic love. Rather it discusses the most important kind of love for marriages (and all other relationships)—that of sacrificial Christian love.

(13:1-3) How does love enhance the other spiritual gifts listed here? Why would love make such a difference?

(13:4-7) What are the qualities of love? How would each of these attributes build up a marriage? How would they build up a congregation? Choose one quality of love to develop in your life during this next week.

(13:8-9) Why might love continue where other gifts cease or disappear? Which of these gifts (love, prophecy, tongues, or knowledge) would have the greatest impact on you? Why?

(13:10-12) Who is Paul speaking of when he writes of the coming perfection? How will we see clearly when that perfection comes?

(13:13) How do you understand the relationship between faith, hope, and love? Why is love the greatest of these?

What idea, verse, or phrase from this chapter can change your experience today?

Day 147
1 Corinthians 14

Background: Again Paul takes a specific topic—speaking in tongues—and expands it into a larger principle. Look for this larger principle as you read. It will apply not only to the situation in Corinth but also to all congregations in every time and place.

(14:1-5) What is necessary for speaking in tongues to be of value to the church (verse 5)? What should be the goal of any spiritual gift? How does speaking in tongues by itself fail to accomplish this goal?

(14:6-12) What do Paul's words suggest for congregations desiring to bring other cultures into their worshiping community? Again, what should be the purpose of all spiritual gifts?

(14:22-25) Why would tongues be a sign for unbelievers but not for believers? Why would the opposite be true for the gift of prophecy? Of whom should congregations be mindful when they gather for worship? How does your congregation make worship meaningful for these people?

(14:26-33) What things does Paul say might be included in worship? Which of these are present in your worship? How do these things strengthen your church? What are you able to contribute to the worship of your congregation? What is it that God desires in worship?

(14:18-21) Read 2 Corinthians 10:10. What is the arrogance that some of the Corinthians show? What is the power that Paul has compared to these individuals?

What idea, verse, or phrase from this chapter can change your experience today?

Day 148
1 Corinthians 15

Background: Paul was very much aware that the Corinthian church was made up of people from many religious backgrounds and beliefs. Some of these beliefs were likely creeping into the beliefs of the Christian church in Corinth. Paul takes time to make sure that they hear again some of the important teachings of Christianity.

(15:1-2) What great gift does the gospel offer? How is this gift received (see also Romans 3:23-24, 28)? What are you doing to hold firm to the word of God that has been proclaimed in your life?

(15:3-11) What resurrection appearances are listed here? Why is the listing of these appearances important to Paul's presentation? What confession does Paul make here? What has he become and how has that happened? What have you become by the grace of God?

(15:12-28) Summarize Paul's argument here. What does it mean that Christ is the first fruits? Why is the resurrection of Christ so important to our Christian faith?

(15:50-57) What is taught here about the resurrection to which we can look forward? In light of this teaching, describe your feelings about death. To whom and for what reason does Paul (and do we) give thanks?

What idea, verse, or phrase from this chapter can change your experience today?

152

Day 149
1 Corinthians 16

Background: Christianity for Jesus and for Paul is never just about taking care of ourselves. Because of a famine in the area of Palestine, Paul regularly encourages the wealthier churches in Asia Minor to send gifts to the poverty-stricken church in Jerusalem. Note that Paul asked nothing for himself (recall chapter 9). However, he has great concern for those in need in other churches.

(16:1-4) What good practice does Paul suggest for providing for the needy in Jerusalem? How does Paul insure that the money will reach its destination? For what needy churches or ministries does your congregation set aside money?

(16:5-12) What do you learn about Paul from these words? What requests does Paul make of the Corinthians? Describe the Christian church in Paul's day. How is the Christian church today like and unlike the first century Christian church?

(16:13-14) How do these words of encouragement sum up this letter? Which one of these will you choose to focus on this week? What will you do to keep it in front of you?

(16:24) In light of his words of instruction in this letter to the Corinthians, why is it significant that Paul sends his personal word of Christian love? What lesson is here for members of all churches?

What idea, verse, or phrase from this chapter can change your experience today?

Day 150
2 Corinthians 1

Background: Paul first visited Corinth on his second missionary trip when the church was founded. On his third missionary trip, Paul had planned to go to Corinth before going to Macedonia and then returning for another visit. When this plan was in place, Paul was on good terms with the Corinthians. Instead, for some reason, Paul paid them a quick visit that apparently was painful for the Corinthians, evidenced by Paul's comments in 1:15-16 and 2:1.

(1:3-7) How does Paul describe God? What does God offer to us? For what purpose do we receive this blessing from God? How are we able to do this? How does this process draw us closer to God? To each other? How does suffering help us grow as Christians?

(1:8-11) Describe Paul's personal experience with suffering. What things supported him in the midst of his suffering? How does the answer to prayer become a witness to others? What prayers has God recently answered in your life?

(1:12-2:4) What do you learn about Paul in these verses? What impresses you most about him?

(1:18-22) How are all God's promises "yes" in Christ? Why are we able to say "amen" or "let it be so" through Christ? What is the seal that God has set upon us?

What idea, verse, or phrase from this chapter can change your experience today?

Day 151
2 Corinthians 2

Background: This second letter to the Corinthians is more likely at least the third in a sequence of letters to the Corinthians with 1 Corinthians being the second (see 1 Corinthians 5:9). Apparently a number of letters went back and forth between Paul and the Corinthian church, including yet another we do not have (see 2 Corinthians 2:4 and 7:8).

(1:23-2:4) What was Paul's goal in the painful visit he made to the Corinthians? How do you think Paul feels about the Corinthians? How does Paul seem to see his relationship with this church?

(2:5-11) From whom does the authority for discipline in the church come? Once that discipline has been given, what should be the response of the church? Why is this response important? What is at risk if we do not respond in this fashion?

(2:12-13) Paul looked for Titus in Troas, hoping to hear news about the Corinthian church. Why was information about Corinth important to Paul? What does Paul mean when he says that in Troas a door was opened? Who created this opening? What does this suggest to you about openings for ministry for you and for your church?

(2:14-17) What is the ultimate source of Paul's joy? Through whom does this good news spread? How are you seeking to spread the "fragrant aroma" of God's love?

What idea, verse, or phrase from this chapter can change your experience today?

Day 152
2 Corinthians 3

Background: One of Paul's agendas in this letter is to address accusations about his credibility. Because Paul had changed his plans to visit Corinth (see 1:15-17), his opponents claimed that none of his messages could be trusted. Beginning in 2:17 and throughout this letter, Paul defends his ministry for Christ.

(3:1-3) In what ways is the Spirit like the ink used to write a letter? How is it different? How are the Corinthians like a letter of recommendation for Paul? How are you like a letter of recommendation for Christ?

(3:4-6) In what ways are we not competent without God? How does God make us competent? How does this answer the question in 2:16? What is the new covenant or promise to which God makes us ministers? What is the "letter" that kills (see Exodus 32:16-16)? How does the Spirit give life?

(3:7-11) Summarize Paul's argument that the new covenant surpasses the law. How is the glory of the law fading away? How does the glory of the new covenant lasting?

(3:12-18) Describe the joy Paul finds in Christ. Why is he able to speak with such confidence? What freedom have you found in Christ? How is God transforming you into the likeness of Christ Jesus? What is one specific way you have become more Christ-like recently?

What idea, verse, or phrase from this chapter can change your experience today?

Day 153
2 Corinthians 4

Background: After having spoken in support of his own ministry, Paul now explains more about Christian ministry in general. The ministry of the gospel is not just for a select few. It is for all. Thus Martin Luther was able to refer to the people of the Christian church as the "priesthood of all believers."

(4:1-6) Who is the god of this world or age? How does this "god" keep unbelievers today from being open to the gospel? What is the focus of Paul's preaching? How does he present himself?

(4:7-12) What is the treasure of which Paul speaks? What are the jars of clay? How is Paul able to find courage in the midst of persecution and suffering? How does Jesus give you courage?

(4:13-15) Why does Paul share the gospel? Based on this reason, who should speak the gospel message to others? How does faith lead to witness? To whom will you witness this week?

(4:16-18) Contrast Paul's physical existence with his spiritual existence. How does God renew you each day? What are the things that are visible? What are the things that are unseen? How do the unseen allow us to keep heart in the midst of the world today?

What idea, verse, or phrase from this chapter can change your experience today?

Day 154
2 Corinthians 5

Background: Throughout 2 Corinthians Paul moves through three important themes. First, the love of God can support us through all trials. Second, through the new covenant in Christ we have new life. Third, having received these undeserved gifts from God, we can respond selflessly and joyfully through the ministry of the gospel and in our support for others.

(5:1-5) What are the earthly and heavenly tents of which Paul speaks? What is Paul's attitude toward earthly things (see also 4:7)? What is it for which Paul longs? Why?

(5:6-10) How does our earthly existence keep us away from the Lord? How is it that, though away from the Lord, we can be confident?

(5:11-15) Why might some understand "fear of the Lord" as dread? Why might some understand it as respect? How do you understand it? If Paul does not commend himself, whom does he commend? Why would this give the Corinthians pride? How would this allow them to challenge those who take pride in the things of this world?

(5:16-21) How has Jesus made you a new creation? What was God's ultimate purpose in sending Christ? How does this make us Christ's ambassadors? What are you doing specifically to be his ambassador?

What idea, verse, or phrase from this chapter can change your experience today?

Day 155
2 Corinthians 6

Background: One of the examples supporting the theory that this letter is a collection of several writings is the section beginning with 6:14 and going through 7:1. If this section were left out, the text flows smoothly from 6:13 into 7:2 and following. Still, the inserted section has as much value for us as it did for the Corinthian congregation.

(6:1-2) What does it mean to work with God? How would one waste the grace of God (see 5:15)? How are you showing the value of God's grace in your life?

(6:3-10) How does Paul try to live his life, even in the midst of hardships and suffering? What traits has he shown in these situations? Why? What surprises you most about these traits? Which one would you most like to develop in your life? Why?

(6:11-13) How does Paul look upon his relationship with the Corinthian church? What is their current attitude toward him? Why does Paul say this should change?

(6:14-18) Why should believers avoid close associations with unbelievers? For what circumstances is Paul giving this instruction (see 1 Corinthians 5:9-11)?

What idea, verse, or phrase from this chapter can change your experience today?

Day 156
2 Corinthians 7

Background: Paul's enemies in Corinth tried to convince his supporters there that Paul did not really care for them. Their goal was to create doubt, first in Paul's affection for them, and then in his message to them. Draw your own conclusions about Paul's feelings for the Corinthian church.

(7:2-4) How do these words support Paul's fatherly image of himself (6:13) toward the Corinthians? From Paul's perspective, are there any grounds for a conflict between him and them? Explain.

(7:5-7) What was Paul's situation when Titus arrived? How did the coming of Titus comfort and encourage Paul? What does this suggest about the importance of Christian relationships? How are you comforting and/or encouraging others?

(7:8-12) What is the relationship between sorrow and repentance? What is the difference between worldly sorrow and godly sorrow? What is the result of godly sorrow? When have you experienced this in your life? How did Paul's letter help the faith of the Corinthians?

(7:13-16) What effect will Paul's words here have on the Corinthians? What lesson is there for churches today? Who in your congregation boasts about the good works of the members?

What idea, verse, or phrase from this chapter can change your experience today?

Day 157
2 Corinthians 8

Background: Paul often stressed to his readers the importance of stewardship, especially with regard to struggling ministries. In the case of his discussion in chapters 8 and 9, Paul is talking about a specific offering he had requested for the church in Jerusalem.

(8:1-7) What is the source of the generosity of the Macedonian churches? What makes their gifts even more significant? What was the first thing given by the Macedonians? What lesson is there for you in this passage?

(8:8-9) Why would Paul not command the Corinthian church to give to this special fund? How is Jesus an example for our giving? How has Jesus made you rich? What perspective does that give you regarding your worldly wealth?

(8:10-15) What attitude makes a gift acceptable in God's eyes? Describe the fair balance that Paul explains.

(8:16-24) What qualities in Titus and "the brother" (probably Luke) are praised by Paul? What example does Paul give for the handling of money by churches? To whom does Paul hold himself accountable in the handling of this money? Why?

What idea, verse, or phrase from this chapter can change your experience today?

Day 158
2 Corinthians 9

Background: Not much is known of the fund about which Paul is talking. It seems to be a special project started by Paul for the church in Jerusalem. They were struggling as a result of famine and of being overly generous in their giving. This fund is mentioned both in 1 Corinthians 16:1-4 (written before this letter) and Romans 15:25-28 (written a few years after this letter).

(9:1-5) What technique did Paul use to motivate both the Corinthian church (Achaia) and the Macedonian church to give? What suggests that Paul felt this gift was important for the spiritual growth of the Corinthians? How has Christian giving helped you to grow spiritually?

(9:6-11) What promises are given to those who "sow generously"? What attitude is necessary for this kind of giving? How can you develop and maintain this attitude in your life? In what special way can you sow generously this week? Ask God to help you do it!

(9:12-15) What blessings come from generous giving? How do you feel knowing that your gifts help supply the needs of God's people? What is the great gift of God for which you give thanks?

What principles for giving are presented in these two chapters?

(8:5)

(9:7)

(8:12)

(8:24)

What idea, verse, or phrase from this chapter can change your experience today?

Day 159
2 Corinthians 10

Background: This last section of 2 Corinthians is probably a separate letter from the first part. In fact, this may be the bitter letter referred to in 7:8. As you read chapters 10-13, decide for yourself if it makes sense that they would have been written after and sent at the same time as chapters 1-9.

(10:1-6) The language Paul uses suggests a very serious situation in Corinth. What are some of those words? What does Paul seek from the Corinthian church (verses 5-6)? What does he threaten?

(10:7-11) Paul's opponents in Corinth used many attacks to discredit him. What suggests that one of these attacks was on Paul's appearance? What other criticism was leveled toward Paul? How does Paul respond to this second criticism?

(10:12-15a) By what standards have Paul's enemies been bragging about themselves and criticizing him? Within what arena does Paul find grounds to boast? What claim can Paul make that his opponents cannot (verse 14)?

(10:15b-18) What reason does Paul give for his words to the Corinthians? What blessing does he hope will result from these efforts? On what basis does Paul claim credibility for his ministry (verse 18)?

What idea, verse, or phrase from this chapter can change your experience today?

Day 160
2 Corinthians 11

Background: Paul now presents a number of arguments supporting his ministry. The sufferings that Paul has experienced give evidence to his commitment to the gospel. Furthermore, they are claims that opponents cannot make. The Corinthians should feel proud that Paul was the one who brought the gospel to them.

(11:1-6) In what ways do you consider yourself "married" to Christ? Is this marriage one you chose or an "arranged marriage"? Explain. What charges does Paul make against the message of those who are speaking against him?

(11:7-12) What things did Paul do when he was with the Corinthians to make sure nothing interfered with the gospel message?

(11:13-15) Who does Paul accuse as false ministers of righteousness in Corinth? What might Satan hope to accomplish through these false teachers? How does Satan disguise himself today?

(11:16-21a) Why does Paul say that boasting about himself is foolishness?

(11:21b-33) What information do you learn about Paul? Does this seem to be boasting? Explain. Why would Paul list his weaknesses rather than strengths? If Paul is contrasting himself against the false apostles, what then are the characteristics of a true apostle?

What idea, verse, or phrase from this chapter can change your experience today?

Day 161
2 Corinthians 12

Background: The "thorn in my flesh" of which Paul speaks in 12:7 remains a mystery to us today. Some have speculated that Paul may have suffered from a physical ailment like epilepsy. Others think this thorn may have been some defect in his outward appearance. Whatever it was, Paul felt that it hampered him in his missionary efforts.

(12:1-6) Apparently, the false teachers in Corinth claimed to receive their teachings directly from God. How does Paul respond to their claims? What is the reality of Paul's boasting (verse 6)?

(12:7-10) In what ways has the "thorn" in Paul's side become a blessing to him? What lesson did Paul learn from this hardship? When have you found God's grace to be sufficient for your trials? How can you use experiences like this to witness to others?

(12:11-18) Who does Paul say is responsible for his need to boast? What things did Paul do in Corinth that apparently the false apostles have not been able to do? What other charge did the false teachers make against Paul and his co-workers? How does Paul defend himself against this charge?

(12:19-21) What has been the sole purpose of Paul's boasting? What do you think are Paul's feelings about the Corinthian church?

What idea, verse, or phrase from this chapter can change your experience today?

Day 162
2 Corinthians 13

Background: Paul mentions that his next visit to Corinth will be his third. His second visit is not mentioned in the history of his travels in Acts. It likely was a very short visit. It also must have been the painful visit mention in 2:1. Paul does not want his next visit to occur with the same need for reprimand as the last one.

(13:1-4) What cautions does Paul say he will take before passing judgment? On what basis does Paul claim his apostolic authority to discipline and punish? In what ways does Paul try to follow the example of Christ Jesus?

(13:5-6) How are the Corinthians to test themselves? Measure yourself in the same way. How do you rate? What will you do today to "raise your score"?

(13:7-10) How would a change in the behavior of the Corinthians make it seem that Paul was a failure? Why would such "failure" make Paul glad? What is the only context for the exercise of Paul's authority? What is to be the goal of all criticism and reprimand?

(13:11-14) What constructive encouragement does Paul give to his readers? What blessing is promised if these instructions are followed? What practice in your congregation is the equivalent of a "holy kiss"?

What idea, verse, or phrase from this chapter can change your experience today?

Day 163
Galatians 1

Background: Galatia was a region that ran north to south through the area that today is central Turkey. Paul traveled through southern Galatia (Antioch, Iconium, Lystra, and Derbe) during his first missionary trip (Acts 13:4-14:28). On his second missionary trip (Acts 15:39—18:22), it is believed that Paul traveled all the way into the northern regions of Galatia, although no specific references are mentioned.

(1:1-5) From what two sources does Paul say his call to this ministry comes? For what two things does Paul credit Christ here? Have you heard this greeting before? If so, where?

(1:6-10) Of what does Paul accuse the Galatians? How does Paul suggest this might be happening? What are some sources of false gospels today? How does the condemnation spoken by Paul here agree with the words of Jesus in Luke 17:1-2? How would trying to win the approval of people make Paul a servant or slave to people? How does his freedom in Christ make him a servant of Christ?

(1:11-12) How did Paul receive the gospel he preaches? What does this suggest to you for those times when you try to witness to others?

(1:13-24) Does it surprise you that Paul is so open about his former life? Why or why not? What effect did his story have on the church in Judea? What story from your life might result in praise of God?

What idea, verse, or phrase from this chapter can change your experience today?

Day 164
Galatians 2

Background: Paul has an important topic to discuss with the congregation in Galatia. Before he begins his presentation on this matter, however, Paul first seeks to establish his authority as an apostle. By doing this, the Galatians will not be able to oppose his argument.

(2:1-3) Why did Paul go to Jerusalem? What was his reason for going there? What does this suggest to you about accountability in the church? How does this happen in your congregation?

(2:4-10) What controversy did Paul face in Jerusalem (verse 3)? What freedom did this threaten? To whom was Paul's ministry primarily directed? To whom was Peter's? Do you have a sense of the ministry to which God has called you? Explain.

(2:11-16) What was the real teaching that Paul challenged against those who required circumcision (verse 16)? Why does Paul say that Peter and James were wrong? In what way did Peter behave as a hypocrite (verse 12)? Does this affect your opinion of Peter? Why or why not?

(2:17-21) How does the law cause one both to die and to live? How would righteousness through the law make Christ death meaningless? How does Christ live in you? How will you let others see Christ in you today?

What idea, verse, or phrase from this chapter can change your experience today?

Day 165
Galatians 3

Background: Abraham is the central figure in this portion of Paul's presentation. Abraham was the physical father of the Jews. Because of his faith in God, Abraham also is the spiritual father of all believers. The Jews believed that it was Abraham's obedience that made him righteous before God. Paul argues that it was his faith.

(3:1-5) How does one receive the Holy Spirit? On what basis are miracles performed? What goal were the Galatians (and you) seeking to reach? What "work" did the Galatians claim was necessary to reach this goal (see 2:3, 12)?

(3:6-9) Who does Paul say are the children of Abraham? Are you one of Abraham's children? Explain. What was the promise God made to Abraham (verse 8)?

(3:15-20) Why do you think Paul refers to Christ as "the Seed"? What is the purpose of the law? When does the law no longer have force?

(3:21-25) What can the law not do? What can it not accomplish? How does the law hold one prisoner to sin? How does it lead one to Christ?

(3:26-29) In what way do people become children of God? Who is included in this unity? Who is excluded?

What idea, verse, or phrase from this chapter can change your experience today?

Day 166
Galatians 4

Background: Paul continues to use significant figures from the Old Testament. In this chapter Sarah, the wife of Abraham, and Hagar, Sarah's handmaiden, are mentioned. It was through Sarah and her son that God's covenant was fulfilled. (Read Genesis 16:1-16 and 21:2-5 to review the events mentioned here.)

(4:1-7) How are we moved from being slaves to the law to children of God? What does this new relationship mean for us? What are we moved to call out when the Spirit of the Son enters our hearts? What does this mean for you?

(4:8-11) To what things that are "not gods" are people enslaved today? What freedom do they seek through these things? How do these things actually enslave them? What makes God different from these "not gods"?

(4:17-20) Again, who are those who are seeking to turn the Galatian Christians away from God's freedom (see 2:4, 12)? What is their goal? About what are you zealous? For what purpose do you have this passion? How do others know of your zeal?

(4:21-31) How are the descendants of Hagar, who did not have the covenant with God, like those who choose to live under the law?

What idea, verse, or phrase from this chapter can change your experience today?

Day 167
Galatians 5

Background: Galatians is very well written in its message that a person is justified by grace alone. It is not by works of the law that a person is made right with God. Rather, obedience to the law comes from faith in Christ that is a gift from God. Even more than the Letter to the Romans, it is this letter that Martin Luther used in his arguments that sparked the Reformation.

(5:1-6) How would giving into the demand for circumcision make Christ of no value to a person? How does turning to the law move a person away from grace? What is the relationship between love and circumcision? Between love and faith?

(5:13-15) What is the freedom that Christians receive? Would you describe the "Golden Rule" (verse 14) as a law? Why or why not? How is love for others different from keeping the law?

(5:16-18) If you have freedom in Christ, why choose not to sin? What puts the Spirit and sinful nature in conflict?

(5:19-26) What vices does Paul list here? What virtues does he list? Which of these virtues will you try to develop this week? In what way do Christians share in Christ's crucifixion? What freedom does that produce? What warning does Paul give to those who know they are free?

What idea, verse, or phrase from this chapter can change your experience today?

Day 168
Galatians 6

Background: Freedom in Christ does not liberate a person from Christian responsibility. Life in Christ connects us to one another in significant ways. Paul does not leave his readers with only half the message. Now he directs them (and us) toward those actions that will give glory to the one who makes us free.

(6:1-5) What warnings does Paul give to his readers? What guidance does he give for Christian relationships? How does Paul emphasize personal responsibility? When do Christians have responsibility for others?

(6:7-10) Put Paul's farming illustration into your own words. How will sowing for the sinful nature lead to a destructive harvest? What are you sowing? What do you hope to reap from these seeds? Why are we to do good especially to other Christians?

(6:12-16) Rather than seeking to make a good impression outwardly, what should Christians pursue? How do you boast in the cross of Jesus Christ? How does God make you a new creation? In what ways is your life different because of being a new creation?

(6:17) For Paul, the marks of Jesus are stoning, beatings, and illnesses he suffered during his ministry. Do you bear any marks of Jesus? If so, what are they?

What idea, verse, or phrase from this chapter can change your experience today?

Day 169
Ephesians 1

Background: Ephesus was the most important city in western Asia Minor (Turkey). It had a harbor and was at a major crossroads of trade routes. It also had a temple to the Roman goddess Diana. According to Acts 19:8-10, Paul evangelized in Ephesus for more than two years.

(1:3-14) This portion of the Letter to the Ephesians is viewed as a doxology because it expresses praise for what God has done. What words or phrases support this position?

(1:3-6) What words are used by Paul to reflect his close relationship to the Ephesians? Does it surprise you that Paul connects himself to the Ephesians in this way? Why or why not? What does this suggest about the relationship between churches?

(1:4-14) How were we chosen by God? What blessings are ours through the Father? For what purpose do we receive these blessings? Which of these blessings have you personally experienced? How are you striving to fulfill God's purpose?

(1:15-23) Name each thing for which Paul prays the Ephesians might receive and the purpose of each blessing:

Blessing	Purpose
(verse 17)	
(verse 18)	

What idea, verse, or phrase from this chapter can change your experience today?

Day 170
Ephesians 2

Background: Having written of the great purpose and plan of God in chapter 1, Paul now explains the steps by which God's plan is accomplished. First, there is human salvation. Next is the reconciliation of Jews and Gentiles, both to God and to each other.

(2:1-10) What is the human condition before knowing Christ? What does this passage tell you about the character of God? What role does Christ play in God's plan? What is human condition after knowing Jesus?

(2:6-10) Put this important message of salvation into your own words. What is the purpose of doing good works?

(2:11-13) What does Paul suggest is the focus of those who emphasize circumcision? What was the former situation of the Gentiles? What is their situation now? How did their situation change?

(2:14-18) How does Paul describe Christ? What did Jesus accomplish? What is the one body Christ has created from two?

(2:19-22) How does Paul describe the church of Christ? What role does Jesus play for the church?

What idea, verse, or phrase from this chapter can change your experience today?

Day 171
Ephesians 3

Background: First God saved people through grace in Christ Jesus and then united them to one another and to God. Now Paul explains more of the nature of the church. Paul talks about this nature as a secret or mystery, revealed to him and to certain others, and now shared with all his readers.

(3:1-6) What is the "mystery" about which Paul writes? Describe the relationship of the Gentiles and the Jews to each other. What is their position in the church?

(3:7-13) What is God's purpose for the church? How are you participating in the accomplishment of this goal? Describe our relationship with God because of our relationship with Christ Jesus.

(3:14-19) Name each thing for which Paul now prays the Ephesians might receive and the purpose of each blessing:

	Blessing	Purpose
(verses 16-17)		
(verse 18)		
(verse 19)		

(3:20-21) What does the power we receive from God afford us? What is the purpose to which God has called the church? How are you working to help your church achieve this purpose?

What idea, verse, or phrase from this chapter can change your experience today?

Day 172
Ephesians 4

Background: Paul has shown very clearly that in Christ, Jews and Gentiles are united into a new relationship called the church. He then wrote of the purpose of the church—to reveal the wisdom of God's plan to others. Now he speaks of the benefits that come to those who live and work together in the community of the church.

(4:1-6) What are the characteristics of those who live the Christian life? What is the goal of this behavior? Identify all the levels of unity that occur within the Christian faith. What is the significance of the order in which Paul lists these levels of unity?

(4:7-13) What do you think Paul means that God has given to each person in proportion? What are some of the gifts God has given? Even though they may not be on this list, what gifts has God given you? How are you using your gifts to build up the body of Christ?

(4:20-24) What does life in Christ challenge a person to do? What kinds of things keep on living the old self? What does the new self look like?

(4:25-32) What are some of the characteristics of the old self? What are the characteristics of the new self? What part of your old self has been most difficult to put off? What trait would you most like to develop? Ask God to sustain you as you seek to become a new creation in Christ.

What idea, verse, or phrase from this chapter can change your experience today?

Day 173
Ephesians 5

Background: Paul showed the unity that comes through God in Christ Jesus for all people. In this chapter and the next he strives to show how new life in Christ can lead to more positive relationships. The example of Christ should serve as a guide for Christians in all aspects of life.

(5:1-2) What is the basis for imitation of Christ? What is the greatest expression of this (see also 4:32)? How will you seek to imitate Christ today?

(5:3-7) Against what things does Paul warn here? What is at risk to the person from such behavior? What might be the reaction of others to seeing these behaviors among Christians?

(5:8-14) What does it mean to live as children of light? What kinds of things might Christians be called to expose with the light of Christ? In what ways are you the light of the Lord?

(5:15-20) For what kinds of opportunities should Christians watch? In what ways does Paul suggest Christians should give thanks to God? How do you do this?

(5:21-33) How are wives to love their husbands? How are husbands to love their wives? What example did Christ set for the marital relationship?

What idea, verse, or phrase from this chapter can change your experience today?

Day 174
Ephesians 6

Background: Some have questioned the authorship of this letter because the usual personal greeting of Paul's other letters is lacking. Furthermore, many parts are quite similar to Colossians, suggesting that someone else copied those portions. It is more likely that this letter was to be read by several churches, including Ephesus.

(6:1-4) How does Paul show that the parent-child relationship (like all relationships) is two-way? Why should children obey their parents? How are parents to raise their children?

(6:5-9) What lessons in the slave-master relationship might apply to life today? In what situations?

(6:10-18) Describe the various pieces of armor and their specific purposes in the spiritual battle against evil. Based on verse 12, how should we understand those occasions when someone does evil to or harms us? How can God's spiritual armor help us in these situations? Beyond putting on the spiritual armor of God, what additionally must one do to be prepared for battle against the powers of evil?

(6:19-20) What is Paul's prayer request for himself? Make this your prayer as well.

What idea, verse, or phrase from this chapter can change your experience today?

Day 175
Philippians 1

Background: The city of Philippi was named for King Philip of Macedonia, the father of Alexander the Great. It was a Roman colony, so all its citizens were also citizens of Rome. They dressed like Romans and spoke Latin, as did the Romans. Many Philippians were retired soldiers who had been given land around the city. In exchange they served as a military presence in this area of the world.

(1:1-2) Three things traditionally were done at the beginning of a letter of this type. Identify each part of the opening in this letter:

Sender:

Recipients:

Greeting:

Compare this opening with that of Hebrews, Titus, James, and Peter.

(1:3-11) What are Paul's feelings toward this congregation? Why does he feel this way? What does Paul pray that might happen among these people?

(1:12-18) What is Paul's situation at the time this letter was written? What different things motivate people to witness for Christ? Why should we not be concerned about the motivations of others? What has motivated you to be courageous in your witness for Christ?

(1:19-26) What are the good alternatives to Paul's current situation? In what situation of your life can these words of Paul sustain you?

What idea, verse, or phrase from this chapter can change your experience today?

Day 176
Philippians 2

Background: Unlike the situation in places such as Corinth or Galatia, Paul is not writing to address a problem in Philippi. His primary reason for writing becomes clear in chapter 4. While he is writing, though, he uses this letter as an opportunity to encourage the Philippians and to commend Timothy and Epaphroditus to them.

(2:1-4) What are the benefits one might enjoy in unity with Christ? Describe the relationship with others that life in Christ can create. Where do you experience these kinds of relationships? What guidelines does Paul give for Christian living?

(2:5-11) How is the attitude of Jesus described in this early Christian hymn? What parallels are there between this hymn and other Christian creeds with which you are familiar?

(2:12-18) What exercises help you "work out" and stay strong in your saving faith? What conduct reflects God working in the life of a Christian? Where do you see God's "shining stars" in the world today? How will you shine today?

(2:19-24) What qualities of Timothy does Paul praise? Who do you know like Timothy? For what might Paul praise you?

What idea, verse, or phrase from this chapter can change your experience today?

Day 177
Philippians 3

Background: Paul uses athletic imagery several times in his letters (see 1 Corinthians 9:24-27; 1 Timothy 6:12; 2 Timothy 4:7-8). There are many similarities between the life of a Christian and the life of an athlete. As in athletics, Christianity involves both individual effort and a commitment to working with the other members of the team.

(3:1) What Christian teachings have you heard repeatedly? How has it been a safeguard for you to hear these over again?

(3:2-6) Summarize Paul's response to those who argue against the preaching of the grace by emphasizing the work of circumcision instead. What "credentials" does Paul present to his readers?

(3:7-11) After presenting his "autobiography" in the preceding verses, what does Paul now say is most important to him? Why does this matter to Paul? What phrases suggest that Paul sees his relationship with Christ as ongoing?

(3:12-14) As you press toward the heavenward goal, what do you need to forget from your past? Thank God who, through the sacrifice of Jesus, has already forgotten.

(3:17-21) What Christians do you know who serve as models for your walk with Christ? Who are the enemies of the cross today?

What idea, verse, or phrase from this chapter can change your experience today?

Day 178
Philippians 4

Background: Paul now finally reaches the main purpose for his letter to the congregation in Philippi: to thank them for their gifts sent to Paul to assist him during his house arrest in Rome (Acts 28:14-31). This unexpected gift gave great joy to Paul, who already had tremendous fondness for these people.

(4:2-3) On what basis are these two women to find common ground in their disagreement (see also 2:1-11)? What role is the congregation to have in this issue? Does your congregation follow this instruction well? Explain.

(4:4-9) Why does Paul say Christians can always be joyful? What practices does Paul encourage his readers to follow? What blessing does Paul promise will follow these behaviors? Does it surprise you that Paul can feel this way while under house arrest? Why or why not?

(4:10-13) What does Paul name as the reason for his joy at this time? How can prosperity be a source of discontent?

(4:14-19) How does Paul describe the financial support of the Philippians? What has their history been in this regard? In what ways does your congregation support the spread of the gospel of Jesus Christ? How do you support this ministry of your church?

What idea, verse, or phrase from this chapter can change your experience today?

Day 179
Colossians 1

Background: A man named Epaphras most likely founded the Christian church in Colossae. Paul probably converted Epaphras during his ministry in Ephesus (Acts 19:10, Colossians 1:7-8). The name Epaphras was a shortened form of Epaphroditus (from Aphrodite, the Greek goddess of love), suggesting that he was formerly a worshiper of that pagan religion.

(1:3-8) Why does Paul thank God for the Colossians? What good news does Paul report about the evangelical mission of the Christian church? What would this suggest about the significance of the Christian message? What is the source of Christian love?

(1:9-14) For what has Paul prayed with regard to the Colossians? Toward what purpose has he offered these prayers? How does Paul show the contrast between life with God and life without God? What blessings do those who live in God's love receive?

(1:15-23) What is the relationship of Christ to God? To creation? To the church? To you? What is Christ's position in history?

(1:24-29) What is Paul's relationship to the church? What duty comes with this calling? How are you carrying out this calling? What is the secret that God has revealed to those who believe in Christ?

What idea, verse, or phrase from this chapter can change your experience today?

Day 180
Colossians 2

Background: Paul writes to the Colossians about issues that threaten the theology of the congregation. Epaphras brought this concern to Paul in Rome. While the false teaching is not named specifically, some of the aspects include rules about food and drink, circumcision, angel worship, and reliance on human wisdom and tradition.

(2:1-5) What is Paul's purpose in this letter? What does Paul want them to know? From what will these "treasures" protect them? What would it mean to you to know that someone you had never met was this concerned about your faith?

(2:6-8) How are you rooted and built up in Christ Jesus? What practices do you follow in order to be strengthened in the faith? For what are you overflowing with thankfulness? How can human traditions and worldly principles take one captive?

(2:9-15) How does life in Christ make one complete? What behaviors occur when one receives life in Christ Jesus? How does the cross disarm the powers and authorities of the world? What specifically will you do today to be dead to sin, but alive to Christ?

(2:16-19) How might false humility or worship of angels threaten one's faith? What is the one connection that will keep faith strong?

What idea, verse, or phrase from this chapter can change your experience today?

Day 181
Colossians 3

Background: A major theme of this letter is the new life that Christians find in Christ Jesus. Like clothing, the old worldly nature is taken off. In place of this old way of living, the convert adopts the behaviors and practices of the Christian life.

(3:1-4) What earthly things will you try to set aside today? What are some "things above" upon which you can set your mind?

(3:5-11) What behaviors are part of the earthly nature? What other behaviors does Paul encourage us to put off? Describe the relationship between people in Christ. How might Paul write verse 11 today?

(3:12-17) What is the "clothing" of God's chosen people? What other practices are Christians instructed to follow? What is the rule under which Christians are to live with each other? On what basis are Christians to speak and act? How do your words and actions give thanks to God?

(3:18-4:1) Describe the attitude with which individuals in Christian households are to have toward one another. What understanding allows a Christian to have this attitude? How does service to Christ help you in your relationships?

What idea, verse, or phrase from this chapter can change your experience today?

Day 182
Colossians 4

Background: One of the individuals who brings this letter to Colossae is a man named Onesimus. Onesimus was a slave (belonging to Philemon, to whom Paul also sends a letter). Paul here says nothing to approves of slavery or support slave revolts. Rather, his comments encourage a Christian approach to the slave-master relationship, perhaps to change the institution from within.

(4:2-4) How have you devoted yourself to prayer? How are alertness and thanksgiving significant to a healthy prayer life? For what church leaders do you pray and what do you ask God to do in their lives?

(4:5-6) What advice does Paul give for our relationships with those outside the church? How are we to make the most of every opportunity? What do you think Paul means when he says our conversation is to be gracious and seasoned with salt?

(4:7-18) What can you learn about Paul's supporters and friends?

Tychicus (see also Ephesians 6:21)

Aristarchus (see also Acts 19:29; 20:4; 27:2)

Mark (see also Acts 12:25; 13:5, 13; 15:36-40; 2 Timothy 4:11)

Demas (see also 2 Timothy 4:10)

Archippus (see also Philemon 2)

What idea, verse, or phrase from this chapter can change your experience today?

Day 183
1 Thessalonians 1

Background: Thessalonica was a busy seaport and the largest city in Macedonia (northeastern Greece today). It was also situated at the crossroads of two major trade routes of the day. The account of the founding of the church is in Acts 17:1-9. This background suggests that some members may have been Jews, although most were Gentile.

(1:1) Why is it significant that these three individuals in particular sent this letter (see Acts 17:1-14)? What does Paul suggest about the relationship between this church and God?

(1:2) Who do you specifically name in your prayers? For what do you thank God about them?

(1:3) What do each of these aspects of Christian life produce?

     Faith:

     Hope:

     Love:

What is the source of these three qualities in Christian life?

(1:4-10) What was the process by which the Thessalonians became Christians? What changes occurred in these people when they received the faith? What effect has their faith had on others? How has the Christian faith changed your life?

What idea, verse, or phrase from this chapter can change your experience today?

Day 184
1 Thessalonians 2

Background: Although it does not seem to be the primary purpose for his writing, Paul ends all of the chapters of this letter with a message of eschatology. Eschatology is the doctrine of last things or end times. Every chapter ends with the promise of the second coming of Christ (1:9-10; 2:19-20; 3:13; 4:13-18; 5:23-24).

(2:1-6) Against what kinds of behaviors is Paul defending himself in this section? What motivates Paul in his witness to the gospel? Whose praise do you seek? What motivates your witness to the gospel?

(2:7-9) What cautions did Paul take when bringing the gospel message to the Thessalonians? What other techniques can you learn from Paul for your witnessing?

(2:10-12) Why might it be helpful for Christians to think of their relationships to the ones to whom they witness like a parent to a child? What behaviors should Christians demonstrate toward the ones they try to reach (and parents toward their children)? Which of these is your strongest ability? Which will you ask God to help you develop more fully?

(2:13-16) In what ways did the Thessalonians become imitators of those in Christ Jesus? In what ways are you an imitator of Christ?

What idea, verse, or phrase from this chapter can change your experience today?

Day 185
1 Thessalonians 3

Background: According to Acts 17:5-10, Paul stayed only a short time in Thessalonica. Because of this, the new Christians in that community were left with little to support them in the midst of persecution. One of Paul's reasons for writing was to encourage these new Christians in their trials.

(3:1-3) How does Paul describe Timothy? What strikes you about that description? What does Timothy's mission to the Thessalonians suggest about the shared nature of God's ministry? When has someone followed up on your God's effort through you? When did God send you to minister after someone else? What were the results of these efforts?

(3:3-5) In what ways are Christians persecuted today? What (or whom) does Paul say is the source of these persecutions? What trials have you suffered for your faith? What danger does Paul imply might result from these temptations?

(3:6-10) What three things about the Thessalonians does Paul consider good news? When has the faith of another encouraged you?

(3:11-13) For what things does Paul pray on behalf of the Thessalonians? For what reason does Paul ask these things?

What idea, verse, or phrase from this chapter can change your experience today?

Day 186
1 Thessalonians 4

Background: Paul recognizes that persecution and trial can turn one away from the Lord. So, Paul urges his readers to continue to strive to live a godly life. Additionally, he encourages them to commit each day to living their lives to the glory of God.

(4:1-2) In verse 1, the word translated "live" can also mean "walk." Why is this second word an appropriate way to describe the Christian life? In what ways are you "walking" in order to please God?

(4:3-8) What caution does Paul give to the Thessalonians? Why should this warning be followed? What do our actions say when we choose not to follow God's will? What do we risk losing?

(4:9-10) For what does Paul commend the Thessalonians? Toward what Christian brothers and sisters beyond your congregation do you show Christian love?

(4:11-12) How can the ordinary practices of daily life earn the respect of those outside the church?

(4:13-18) Describe the process by which the faithful, both dead and alive, will enter into eternal life with Christ.

What idea, verse, or phrase from this chapter can change your experience today?

Day 187
1 Thessalonians 5

Background: Paul uses the metaphor of armor in several of his letters (see also Romans 13:12; 2 Corinthians 6:7; 10:4, Ephesians 6:13-17). The image of being prepared with the equipment of Christianity is especially profound for this congregation that is regularly persecuted because of their faith in Christ Jesus.

(5:1-3) What do Paul's words (and Jesus' words in Luke 12:39) suggest about those who claim to have insight into the date of our Lord's return? What does it mean for your life that Jesus might return anytime? Is this comforting knowledge for you or frightening? Why?

(5:4-11) What instructions are given to those who wait for the Lord? Why do Christians need not worry about the "thief " who comes in the night? What are the three tools of the Christian? When has the hope of salvation led you to encourage other Christians?

(5:12-22) What instructions does Paul give you about the leaders in the church? Who are the leaders in your church? What are we to do in relationship to others in the church? What instruction does Paul give for each Christian? Which of these is most difficult for you? Why?

(5:23-24) What is the origin of sanctity of each believer? What is Paul's prayer for each believer? How can this happen?

What idea, verse, or phrase from this chapter can change your experience today?

Day 188
2 Thessalonians 1

Background: Paul's second letter to the church in Thessalonica appears to have been written not long (perhaps six months) after the first letter. It addresses many of the same issues as the first letter, indicating that the situation in this congregation has not changed much. While there are ten words not used elsewhere in the New Testament and some differences in style, most scholars still hold to Paul as the author.

(1:3-4) What reasons does Paul give for his boasting about the Thessalonians? Could Paul say the same things about your congregation? Why or why not? For what other reasons might someone boast about your congregation?

(2:5-10) What things does this passage teach about the nature and behavior of God? Of Jesus? What is the relationship between God and Jesus? What hope and encouragement does Paul give to the Thessalonians in the midst of their persecutions? What is in store for those who do not believe in the one God? What does this suggest to you about the need to share the gospel with others?

(1:11-12) Can God count you worthy of the calling of Christian? Why or why not? What good purposes of yours are you trusting that God will fulfill? What significance does the name of Jesus have for you? In what ways is the name of Jesus glorified in you?

What idea, verse, or phrase from this chapter can change your experience today?

Day 189
2 Thessalonians 2

Background: Once again, Paul addresses the second coming of Christ with the Thessalonians. Now, though, he expands on his previous writing and shares more about the final days of this age. One portion of this has to do with the "man of lawlessness," a term mentioned nowhere else in Scripture.

(2:1-4) What does Paul mention that suggests a reason for his writing this letter? What caution does Paul give to us as we wait for the return of Christ? What sign will precede the second coming of Christ? What hope does Paul offer in light of this sign?

(2:5-12) In what places do you see Satan at work in the world today? What holds Satan in check today? What is the behavior that causes some to perish?

(2:13-15) What two gifts of God lead to salvation? Through what medium did God call the Thessalonians to faith? Through what medium did God call you? What practice will help us to remain solid in our faith?

(2:16-17) Compare this prayer with that in 1 Thessalonians 3:12-13. How are they similar? How are they different? What parts of these two prayers would you ask for your church? Why?

What idea, verse, or phrase from this chapter can change your experience today?

Day 190
2 Thessalonians 3

Background: A final topic that Paul addresses with the Thessalonians (as he did in 1 Thessalonians 4:11-12; 5:14) is that of laziness. It seems that some Christians in Thessalonica were claiming at least that they did not need to work, and perhaps even that the church should care for them. Paul is very concerned that Christians do not see themselves as deserving of special privileges.

(3:1-5) When have you asked for special prayers? From whom did you ask them? Why did you seek prayer? What was the result of the prayers on your behalf?

(3:6-10) What was Paul's behavior during his time among the Thessalonians? Why was it important that he chose to live in this fashion? What lesson is here for you? How are you following this teaching?

(3:11-13) What behavior does Paul criticize as being worse than idleness? Does it surprise you that this behavior comes out of idleness? Explain. How might this behavior impact the congregation?

(3:14-15) What instruction does Paul give for discipline in the church? With what attitude is this action to be taken?

What idea, verse, or phrase from this chapter can change your experience today?

Day 191
1 Timothy 1

Background: 1 and 2 Timothy and Titus were written by Paul to two of his closest and most trusted assistants. They are called pastoral letters because they give instruction to Timothy and Titus about the pastoral care of churches. Timothy was assigned to train pastors in the care of the church in Ephesus (1 Timothy 1:3) and Titus was commissioned to do the same in Crete (Titus 1:5; 2:15; 3:12-13).

(1:3-11) Why was it necessary for Timothy to "pastor" the church in Ephesus? What was to be the motivation for Timothy's leadership in this church? What is the source of this motivation? What does Paul tell us about the law? For whom is it given? How does one know if a teaching is sound doctrine?

(1:12-14) How does this section explain Paul's understanding of the use of the law? How was Paul changed? What impression would it make upon you to see this kind of change in another? What changes can others see in you because of your faith and love in Jesus Christ?

(1:15-17) Can you apply "The saying is sure and worthy of full acceptance" to your own life? Explain. When has Christ Jesus shown his unlimited patience to you? How can that be an example to others?

What idea, verse, or phrase from this chapter can change your experience today?

Day 192
1 Timothy 2

Background: Timothy was a native of Lystra (in modern Turkey). His father was Greek and his mother was a Jewish Christian (Acts 16:1). Timothy joined Paul on his second missionary trip (Acts 16:3) and was with Paul in Macedonia and Achaia (Acts 17:14-15; 18:5) and in Ephesus (Acts 19:22). He traveled extensively with Paul (Acts 20:1-6) and was with Paul during his imprisonment (Philippians 1:1; Colossians 1:1; Philemon 1).

(2:1-2) What types of prayer does Paul encourage for worship? For whom should congregations be praying? What does Paul say is the objective of all these kinds of praying? When in worship does your congregation pray? What types of prayer are included? For whom does your church pray?

(2:3-6) What is God's ultimate desire for humanity? How does this compare with Jesus' final words to his followers in Matthew 28:19-20?

(2:8) With what attitude should we enter into prayer? Compare this teaching with that of Jesus in Matthew 5:23-24.

(2:8-15) What is Paul's attitude about worship? What is one of the primary roles of worship (verse 11)?

What idea, verse, or phrase from this chapter can change your experience today?

Day 193
1 Timothy 3

Background: Two important church leadership roles are discussed in this chapter. The term *bishop* refers to a presiding official in a civic or religious organization. The term *deacon* means, literally, "one who waits on tables." It refers to those who are appointed to serve in the church. Their service seeks to handle details in the church that might prevent the elders from giving full attention to prayer and leadership of the worshiping community (see Acts 6:1-6).

(3:1-7) What qualifications are listed here for bishops?

(3:8-12) What qualifications are given for deacons?

(3:1-12) Which of these qualities do you possess? Which do you need to cultivate? On which one will you concentrate this week? How are you using your gifts in leadership roles in your church?

(3:15) In what ways is the church described here? Why would appropriate conduct be important in the church?

(3:16) Who is the "mystery" or "secret" referred to in this early Christian hymn? Is mystery or secret an appropriate term for this person? Explain.

What idea, verse, or phrase from this chapter can change your experience today?

Day 194
1 Timothy 4

Background: Paul instructs Timothy in dealing with false teachings. Among the false teachings given in Ephesus was that of asceticism. This heresy tried to direct new Christians to a strict lifestyle that involved abstaining from many practices in the church. The danger in the teaching was that it could move new believers away from a relationship based on faith to one of works.

(4:1-5) What deceiving spirits are active in the world today? What specific instructions do the false teachers in Ephesus give? Why does Paul say these teachings are wrong?

(4:6-8) If a leader is going to correct those who follow or give false teachings, what must the leader first do? Do you give as much attention to your spiritual fitness as to your physical fitness? Why or why not? Of what does your current weekly spiritual workout consist?

(4:9-10) To whom does God offer salvation? For whom is that salvation realized?

(4:11-14) Why does Paul say Timothy might encounter opposition? What personal instructions does Paul give to Timothy? Why are these directives important for the effectiveness of Timothy's ministry? Will others respect your efforts in Christ's name because of the way you live? Explain.

What idea, verse, or phrase from this chapter can change your experience today?

Day 195
1 Timothy 5

Background: The Christian life is not only about doctrinal teachings and developing a strong personal faith. Life in Christ also calls us into relationships with other Christians. Knowing how to relate to the various groups of people with whom one must live in the church is very important for the life and growth of the congregation.

(5:1-2) Why does treating one another as family members make sense for the building up of the church? What do you think Paul means to treat one another with absolute purity?

(5:3-8) Summarize Paul's teaching about the responsibility that comes with family relationships. Where do your family responsibilities lie? What danger lies in the pursuit of pleasure? How does negligence of family responsibilities reflect a denial of faith?

(5:9-10) The list apparently was a roster of widows maintained by the church. Why would it be necessary for the church to have such a list (recall verses 3-8)? How might Paul's recommendations regarding this list help to build up the church?

(5:17-20) What responsibility does the church have to those who serve the church as pastors and staff? How should congregations handle accusations against a church leader? Why is this an important directive for the health of a congregation?

What idea, verse, or phrase from this chapter can change your experience today?

Day 196
1 Timothy 6

Background: As one reads this letter, the impression is that Paul is writing specifically to Timothy. His closing words ("Grace be with you"), however, are written in the plural. This suggests that though the letter was written to Timothy, Paul's intention was that it be read to the entire congregation.

(6:1-2) How might these words apply to the relationship between employee and employer? Why might a believer treat another believer in a position of authority with less respect? How does serving a fellow believer better reflect a sense of mission?

(6:3-5) What does Paul say motivates those who stir up controversy in a congregation? Have you ever seen this to be true? If so, when?

(6:6-10) How can the desire for wealth lead one away from faith? How can a believer find contentment in what he or she has? For what are you grateful to God?

(6:11-16) Which of the pursuits toward which Paul directs Timothy is your greatest pursuit? Which is your strongest? How are you "fighting the good fight"? How is God helping you in this good fight? When did you make your "good confession" of faith?

What idea, verse, or phrase from this chapter can change your experience today?

Day 197
2 Timothy 1

Background: The second letter to Timothy is the last written document of Paul's preserved today. He is no longer living in a rented house (Acts 28:30)—as Paul writes this letter, he is chained (2 Timothy 1:16) in a prison (2 Timothy 4:13). Paul understands that his life's work is nearly done and his life is near its end (2 Timothy 4:6-8).

(1:3) How can Paul write these words considering his current situation? Have you been able to give thanks to God in the midst of trial or suffering? Why or why not?

(1:5-7) Who were those whose faith served as an example for the development of your faith? Who are you mentoring in the faith? What gifts has God given you for ministry? How are you fanning these gifts into flame?

(1:8-12) Does it seem odd to you that a believer would be ashamed of another who suffers for the gospel? Explain. How is it that Paul reminds us we are saved? From where does grace come? What does Paul say that Christ has accomplished for us?

(1:13-14) To what is it that Paul encourages us to hold? What does it mean that God has entrusted you with this? What are you doing to honor that trust?

What idea, verse, or phrase from this chapter can change your experience today?

Day 198
2 Timothy 2

Background: Paul writes to Timothy to encourage him again in his work with the church in Ephesus. Apparently heresies continue to be a problem. The one that is mentioned in this chapter seems to be an early form of Gnosticism. Gnosticism taught that the body was evil and the soul, good. This heresy denied the resurrection of the body, since only the good soul would be saved.

(2:3-6) How is each of these a good analogy for the Christian life?

Soldier (3-4):

Athlete (5):

Farmer (6):

(2:11-13) What is Paul's point in quoting this early Christian hymn?

(2:14-15) What is the tool of the Christian worker? How are you using this tool? What are you doing to improve your skill with it?

(2:22-26) What are the characteristics of the Christian servant? How can these characteristics in you influence the lives and faith of others?

What idea, verse, or phrase from this chapter can change your experience today?

Day 199
2 Timothy 3

Background: A primary concern of Paul in this second letter to Timothy and the church at Ephesus is to encourage them in times of persecution and in the last days. Paul's concern is that his readers not lose faith in times of great trial when fear for one's life and temptation toward the worldly may lead a believer to lose his or her faith.

(3:1-5) Do you see evidence of this "last days behavior" in the world today? If so, where? What do those who pursue these behaviors reveal themselves to be? What is Paul's recommendation to us with regard to those who seek these worldly practices? Should we not seek to bring the gospel to these people? Explain.

(3:6-9) What are some of the activities of those who oppose the truth of God? What will be God's response to them?

(3:10-13) What did Paul experience as a result of his ministry of sharing the gospel (see Acts 13:14-14:23; 16:1-6)? Do Paul's words in verse 12 concern you? Why or why not? How did God respond to Paul's persecutions?

(3:14-17) How does Paul describe Scripture? Who introduced you to the Scriptures? Why should a believer continue to study the Scriptures? For what can the Scriptures be used?

What idea, verse, or phrase from this chapter can change your experience today?

Day 200
2 Timothy 4

Background: The names of those whom Paul mentions in this chapter say a great deal about the significance of Paul's ministry in the history of the Christian church. Among those mentioned are Titus, whom Paul assigned to "pastor" the congregation on Crete and to whom he wrote a pastoral letter; Luke, who wrote a gospel of Jesus Christ and the book of Acts; and Mark, who wrote what is considered the oldest gospel of Jesus Christ in the Bible.

(4:1-5) What specific charges does Paul give to Timothy? What warning does Paul give about the future? Does this warning seem an apt description of the world today? Explain. What does Paul say Timothy should do when these days come?

(4:6-8) How do you react to this "funeral sermon" Paul preaches for himself? Does it seem a good description for Paul? Why or why not? Could the same things be said for you? Explain. How are you now fighting the good fight? What is the race you are striving to finish? What are you doing to keep the faith?

(4:14-18) Why would Paul pass sentence on Alexander the metal worker but ask forgiveness for those who deserted him? What did Paul seek to do in the midst of his trials? How are you seeking to proclaim the gospel message? Since Paul expects to die soon (verse 6), what is the rescue he anticipates from God?

What idea, verse, or phrase from this chapter can change your experience today?

Day 201
Titus 1

Background: Titus played a key supportive role in Paul's ministry. He was one of Paul's converts (Titus 1:4). Titus accompanied Paul when he went to Jerusalem to discuss his ministry to the Gentiles (Galatians 2:1-5). The acceptance of Titus as an uncircumcised Gentile cleared the way for Paul's ministry to the Gentile communities.

(1:1-4) Compare this salutation with those at the beginning of Romans, Galatians, and Philippians. How are they the similar? How are they different?

(1:1-3) How does God (verse 2) compare with the Cretans (verse 12)? How have you seen God working in God's own time and not according to worldly expectations? How was the Word brought to light in your life?

(1:5-9) What characteristics does Paul seek in elders or bishops? What does the term elder suggest to you about the qualifications of the person? What does bishop suggest about the work of the person?

(1:10-14) What behaviors and practices in Crete did Paul assign Titus to address? Why was the danger if these things were not corrected? What was to be the goal of this correction?

What idea, verse, or phrase from this chapter can change your experience today?

Day 202
Titus 2

Background: Crete is the fourth largest of the Mediterranean islands. Apparently, Paul was the first to bring the Christian message to Crete. When he had to leave, Paul assigned Titus the task of completing the ministry Paul had started there. At the time this letter was written, the population of Crete had given into many deplorable practices. Paul's goal is to assist Titus in remedying this situation.

(2:2-5) What conduct is Titus to encourage in the older members of the Cretan church? Why is such conduct important in a community of faith? What do the older members teach the younger members in your congregation? What, if any, behaviors on the part of the older members should be corrected?

(2:6-8) What do verses 6-7 suggest about Titus? How does the Cretan church seem to view Titus? Do Paul's instructions to Titus here apply only to the younger men in the church? Explain.

(2:2-10) What do all these teachings suggest about the responsibility that each member of a Christian community has toward the others? How is this lived out in your church? How are you seeking to set an example for others in your church?

(2:11-14) How do these words apply to what was said in the previous verses of this chapter?

What idea, verse, or phrase from this chapter can change your experience today?

Day 203
Titus 3

Background: Paul repeatedly stresses the importance of doing what is good. This may seem to suggest that good works are important for salvation. Rather, the focus is on works as response to what God has already accomplished in one's life. Good works reflect the believer's commitment to do what God desires because of what God has done, and as an example to others.

(3:1-2) How can subjecting oneself to those in authority show greater submission to God? What other behaviors does Paul encourage? How might these practices impact those in authority?

(3:3-8) What contrast does Paul show between himself and God? What is the work of the Savior? What is the work of the Holy Spirit? How does God achieve the salvation of the individual?

(3:9-11) How does Paul say to deal with those who seek to divide the church? How might continued debate harm the church? What are the goals of those who seek to divide (see 1 Timothy 6:3-5)?

(3:12-15) What is taught here about the nature of the church? What Christians outside your congregation are cared for directly by the ministrations of your church? What responsibilities do churches have for spreading the gospel outside their community or area?

What idea, verse, or phrase from this chapter can change your experience today?

Day 204
Philemon

Background: Paul wrote this letter to Philemon, a slave owner in Colossae. Onesimus, one of Philemon's slaves, had apparently stolen from Philemon and then run away. Under Roman law, this was a crime punishable by death. Onesimus became a Christian through Paul's teachings and agreed to return to his master.

(4-7) For what does Paul commend Philemon? How does actively sharing one's faith help the believer to better understand what Christ has provided? Have you experienced this? If so, when?

(8-10) Why does Paul allow Philemon to make his own choice about Onesimus, instead of commanding him? On what basis does Paul encourage Philemon to make his decision? How does Paul describe himself and, indirectly, Philemon?

(11-16) Onesimus means "useful." What contrast does Paul make with the meaning of Onesimus' name to influence Philemon? How has conversion changed Onesimus? How has this change in Onesimus altered his relationship with Philemon?

(17-18) How does Paul's request here mirror what Christ has done for all Christians? If Christ has done this for you, what then can you hold against another?

What idea, verse, or phrase from this chapter can change your experience today?

Day 205
Hebrews 1

Background: The Letter to the Hebrews was written to Jewish converts to Christianity who were being tempted to revert to Judaism. These early Christians were quite familiar with the Old Testament. Thus many Old Testament quotations are used to support the arguments made in favor of the worship of and faith in Jesus Christ.

(1:1-2) In what ways has God attempted to communicate God's love to humankind? What does this tell you about both the Old Testament and the New Testament of the Bible?

(1:2-3) What seven descriptive statements does the writer make about Jesus? What does this suggest about the message of Jesus compared to the message of the prophets (verse 1)? What is the significance of Jesus who "sat down at the right hand of the Majesty on high?" Why is this an important point to make to those considering a return to Judaism?

(1:4-7, 13) What do these passages reveal about the Christ's relationship to God the Father? What does the author say about the angels? How does the author show the superiority of Jesus to the angels?

(1:8-12) What things does the writer reveal about the Son of God?

What idea, verse, or phrase from this chapter can change your experience today?

Day 206
Hebrews 2

Background: Until about 1600 A.D., it was commonly held that the writer of this letter was Paul. The writing style, however, and the statement in 2:3 make it clear that Paul was not the author. The writer of Hebrews was well known, had authority from the early church, and was a Hebrew Christian. Barnabas has been suggested as one possibility. Martin Luther was the first to suggest Apollos, and this is the favorite choice of most scholars today.

(2:1-4) What warning does the author give here? What is the angels' message, referred to in verse 2? What was the consequence of ignoring this message? What greater message has been given than that of the angels? How has God supported the importance of this latter message?

(2:5-8) What place has God given to human beings in the order of creation?

(2:9, 14-18) Why did Jesus become human? Why did he have to suffer death? What does it mean to you that Jesus was tested?

(2:10-13) What was accomplished by Jesus' death? What new relationship do those who believe in Jesus receive? How do you experience this new relationship?

What idea, verse, or phrase from this chapter can change your experience today?

Day 207
Hebrews 3

Background: The Letter to the Hebrews contains five warnings. These warnings are placed at key points throughout the letter. They occur at 2:1-4; 3:7-4:13; 5:11-6:12; 10:19-39; and 12:14-29. These warnings serve as practical behaviors for those who are Christians. They are especially important for those who are tempted to stray from the Christian life back to previous belief systems.

(3:1) What is the heavenly calling? Why is "apostle" a good description for Jesus (see 2 Corinthians 12:12)? How do you understand the responsibilities of the high priest of the Jewish temple (see Leviticus 16:15-17)? Why is Jesus called our high priest?

(3:1-6) Why is the comparison of Christ with Moses important in this letter? What is the "house" that Jesus built? What was the role of Moses in the house?

(3:12-15) Summarize the warning given in this section. How can sin harden a person's heart? How can you encourage someone today to remain strong in the faith?

(3:7-11, 16-19) What happened to the people who followed Moses? Why did this happen? What then could be the consequences to those who give into unbelief?

What idea, verse, or phrase from this chapter can change your experience today?

Day 208
Hebrews 4

Background: This chapter begins a significant discussion of the superiority of Jesus and what he accomplished to that of the Hebrew priesthood. The author of Hebrews strives to show that the Old Testament system of sacrifice is lesser to the sacrifice of Jesus Christ. Jesus' perfect sacrifice has replaced the need for any kind of sacrifice.

(4:1-2) What is God's promise that remains available? How is it that one receives this promise? Why did those who followed Moses in the desert not receive the promise? What are you doing make this promise a reality in your life?

(4:6-7) What was the disobedience of those who did not receive the promise of God (see 3:18-19)? How did God respond to this disobedience? What does this mean for you?

(4:12-13) How is the proclaimed word of God described here? When have you experienced the two-edged sword of God in your life? How is God described in these verses? How are God and God's word the same?

(4:14-16) If Jesus is our high priest, what does heaven represent (read Leviticus 16:15-17)? Why can Jesus sympathize with our struggle against sin? What does this mean for you personally? What do we receive when we draw near to Christ? When do you experience this?

What idea, verse, or phrase from this chapter can change your experience today?

Day 209
Hebrews 5

Background: The writer of Hebrews presents Jesus as the great high priest until the middle of chapter 10. Jesus is not like Moses leading us through the wilderness. He is the high priest who enters the Holy of Holies in the temple to make sacrifice for the sins of the people. However, the sacrifice Jesus offers is not an animal; it is himself.

(5:1-4) What two things were necessary for the selection of a high priest? What are the duties and characteristics of the high priest? What must the high priest first do before making sacrifice for the sins of the people he represents?

(5:4-6) In Jesus' day, the office of high priest was purchased from the Roman government. How did Jesus Christ's role as our high priest fulfill God's original intent for this position?

(5:7-10) What qualifications does Jesus bring to the office of high priest? What about this description of Jesus makes you want him as your high priest? How does Jesus go beyond the ordinary responsibilities of the high priest?

(5:11-14) What might cause a Christian to remain, spiritually, like an infant? What is one behavior that signifies maturity in the faith? Are you more like a teacher or an infant in the Christian faith? Explain.

What idea, verse, or phrase from this chapter can change your experience today?

Day 210
Hebrews 6

Background: Verses 4-6 of this chapter comprise a difficult passage to understand. There are three possible interpretations: 1) It is speaking about Christians who actually lose their faith; 2) It is a warning designed to encourage immature Christians to strive for maturity; or 3) It is talking about those who commit apostasy—that is, those who, having received faith through the Holy Spirit, intentionally reject salvation.

(6:1-3) What are the six basic teachings of Christian faith listed here? How do you understand each of these?

(6:4-6) What are the various events or perspectives experienced by those who convert to Christianity? What physical senses are used to describe these delights of the experience of conversion? What feelings did you experience when the faith became real for you?

(6:9-12) What behaviors can help one to continue toward Christian maturity? How is the example of others important for faith development? Who are you encouraged to imitate?

(6:13-20) What are the two unchangeable things God made (verse 17)? What was God's promise to Abraham? What is God's promise to you? How is this an anchor for you?

What idea, verse, or phrase from this chapter can change your experience today?

Day 211
Hebrews 7

Background: Melchizedek, a Canaanite (Genesis 14:18-20), was the king and high priest of Salem (a shortened form of Jerusalem). In non-Israelite cities, the same person often carried out the duties of both king and priest. This was different than the priestly duties of Aaron, the brother of Moses, who had no political responsibilities.

(7:1-3) What about Melchizedek allows the author of Hebrews to use him a good comparison for Jesus? What does Abraham's response to Melchizedek suggest (see also verse 5)?

(7:4-10) Describe the relationship between Melchizedek and Abraham. What evidence is given for the superiority of Melchizedek to Abraham? What would this say to the Hebrew readers of this letter (see 6:13-15)? What does this then suggest about Jesus?

(7:11-19) What is the significance of the recognition of Melchizedek as the beginning of a new order? How is Jesus the beginning of a new order? Why was this necessary?

(7:20-28) What are Jesus' qualifications to serve as our high priest? What weaknesses do those who live under the law of the levitical priests show? What is the strength that comes from living under Jesus the Son?

What idea, verse, or phrase from this chapter can change your experience today?

Day 212
Hebrews 8

Background: Take a moment to read Jeremiah 31:31-34. The next section of Hebrews is based on this passage of scripture that talks about the new covenant Jesus brings. This is the new covenant referred to in Hebrews 7:22. Not only does Jesus establish or mediate this new covenant, he guarantees it through the sacrifice of his own flesh and blood.

(8:1-2) Read Leviticus 16:2, 13-15, 34. How often was the high priest to enter the tabernacle? What was he to do there? How does this differ from Jesus, our high priest?

(8:3-6) What is important about the point that Jesus is not on earth? What words show that the earthly sanctuaries are inferior to the heavenly sanctuary? What sacrifice did Jesus make and what are the gifts that he offers? Say a prayer to Jesus, thanking him for these tremendous blessings.

(8:6-7) Summarize the main point of these verses.

(8:8-12) Why is the new covenant necessary? What are the characteristics of the new covenant? How will this covenant change things for those who live under it? How will our relationship with God be different under this covenant?

What idea, verse, or phrase from this chapter can change your experience today?

Day 213
Hebrews 9

Background: Again, both the writer of the Letter to the Hebrews and the first readers obviously have great familiarity with the Old Testament and the practices of the Hebrew faith. The writer makes many references to the practices of worship in the Jewish temple. These are spelled out in great detail in the books of Exodus, Leviticus, and Numbers of the Old Testament.

(9:1-5) Under whose leadership was this earthly sanctuary set up (see verse 8:5)? Remembering what was said about the earthly sanctuary compared to the heavenly one in chapter 8, what does this say about this leader in comparison to the leadership Jesus offers?

(9:6-10) What were the specific practices of the high priest under the old covenant? What was the purpose of these practices? Why were they not effective in accomplishing their purpose?

(9:11-15) What sacrifice was offered by Jesus, our high priest? How is the sacrifice of Jesus superior to the sacrifice made by the Hebrew high priests? What does this sacrifice bring to those who live under the new covenant?

(9:24-28) What more is Jesus able to do on our behalf that a high priest is not able to do? What does this mean for us?

What idea, verse, or phrase from this chapter can change your experience today?

Day 214
Hebrews 10

Background: The Letter to the Hebrews is one of the finest documents of encouragement in Christian history. The author has great concern that his readers will slip away from the Christian faith. In this chapter, he finishes his persuasive argument of why the sacrifice of Christ was necessary. He then follows with an encouragement for his readers to persevere in their pursuit of a meaningful relationship with God.

(10:1-3, 11-14) How effective is the sacrifice of the high priests compared to the sacrifice of Jesus? Explain. What is the meaning of the contrast between standing and sitting (verses 11-12)?

(10:19-25) How is it that we now have access to the sanctuary? Read Mark 15:38. Why is the curtain of the sanctuary presented as the body of Christ? What five things are we encouraged to do as a result of our access to the sanctuary?

(10:22) What four conditions are given for drawing near to God? Review yourself under each of these conditions.

(10:32-39) Have you ever experienced insult or persecution for your faith? If so, when? When, if ever, have you defended or supported another who was sharing the gospel? How can faith in Christ give a person confidence in the face of such persecution?

What idea, verse, or phrase from this chapter can change your experience today?

Day 215
Hebrews 11

Background: The next large section of this letter (11:1-12:29) consists of a series of appeals based on the information already gleaned from the Old Testament. Using faith examples from Israel's history, the author attempts to encourage his Hebrew readers to hold to the faith that is even greater than the best known from Israel's past.

(11:4-40) What actions were taken by the following people because of faith?

Abel:

Enoch:

Noah:

Abraham:

Isaac:

Jacob:

Joseph:

Moses' parents:

Moses:

The people of Israel:

Rahab:

What is the relationship between faith and action?

What idea, verse, or phrase from this chapter can change your experience today?

Day 216
Hebrews 12

Background: The city of Jerusalem, built on Mount Zion, was and is the center of political and religious life for Israel. For the early Christian community, Jerusalem came to represent the possibilities of heaven. Paul wrote of the earthly and heavenly Jerusalem in Galatians in 4:25-26. In the Book of Revelation, Mount Zion is the dwelling place of the Lamb (Revelation 14:1) and the New Jerusalem descends to earth as the home of those saved in Christ.

(12:1-3) How is staying solid in faith like running an athletic race? What sin entangles and hinders you in your race? What advice does the author of Hebrews give for you in this struggle?

(12:4-11) What does discipline from God show about our relationship with God? What is the purpose of God's discipline? What hardships have served as God's discipline in your faith life?

(12:14-15) What additional purpose is given here for striving to live a life of faith? What can happen if we do not?

(12:18-24) What are the characteristics of Mount Sinai where Moses received the Ten Commandments? What are the characteristics of Mount Zion where God offers the new covenant? How are God and Jesus described?

What idea, verse, or phrase from this chapter can change your experience today?

Day 217
Hebrews 13

Background: With the argument of Hebrews completed with great flair in chapter 12, chapter 13 seems almost out of place. It is a broad collection of encouragement and advice. Some have suggested it was attached to the original letter to support the author as Paul. In any case, it still has much to offer Christian readers.

(13:1-6) What five virtues are encouraged in this section? What do they suggest about life in the Christian community? How does this behavior encourage growth in faith?

(13:9-10) What can anchor you so you are not carried away by strange teachings (see Hebrews 6:19)? Through what means do you receive God's gracious love and forgiveness?

(13:15-16) What kind of sacrifice through Jesus Christ has replaced the animal sacrifices of the law? When do you offer this type of sacrifice? How is service to others a form of sacrifice to God? In what ways are you making this form of sacrifice?

(13:20-21) How do these verses relate to verse 18-19? How did God establish peace for us? What is the significance of Jesus as the great Shepherd of the sheep? With what has the great Shepherd equipped you for doing his will?

What idea, verse, or phrase from this chapter can change your experience today?

Day 218
James 1

Background: The Letter of James is addressed to "the twelve tribes in the Dispersion." This suggests that the recipients were Jewish Christians who, following the martyrdom of Stephen (Acts 7:54-60), dispersed into many parts of the world (Acts 8:1-3). This understanding of the recipients is supported by Old Testament references and some Hebrew terms (such as "Lord of hosts" in 5:4).

(1:2-8) Why can the testing of your faith be a source of joy for Christians? What are the results of these trials? How is prayer a key part of Christian maturity? What must one be able to do before asking God for help? What is essential to our prayers?

(1:12-18) How does perseverance in time of trial reflect love for God? What is the source of temptation? How then can trial and temptation lead to maturity of faith? When has God brought a "perfect gift" into your life through an experience of temptation or trial?

(1:15) What three stages are given here for the effect of temptation? How can these stages be seen in 2 Samuel 11:2-17?

(1:19-27) What recommendations does James give for Christian living? Explain the illustration of the mirror. What is the relationship between our words and our actions?

What idea, verse, or phrase from this chapter can change your experience today?

Day 219
James 2

Background: The Letter of James has been criticized for emphasizing works over faith as the way into heaven. The faith that he denounces in this chapter is barren (verse 20) and dead (verses 17, 26). It simply accepts certain truths without life-changing trust in Christ. True saving faith produces good deeds, but it is faith, alone, that saves.

(2:1-7) What warning does James give to his readers? What danger lies in not following this caution? In what other ways do churches or church members discriminate? Do you consider yourself to be more rich in the eyes of the world or rich in faith? Explain.

(2:8-11) What is to be our motivation in every action? How does showing partiality violate this? How can something as minor as showing partiality be equated with adultery and murder?

(2:12-13) How does the law give freedom? What reward will be given to those who show mercy?

(2:14-18) What is the relationship between works and faith? How are works a sign of genuine faith? Does this mean that works are essential for salvation (see Romans 3:28)?

(2:20-24) What effect did works have on Abraham's faith?

What idea, verse, or phrase from this chapter can change your experience today?

Background: James was most likely the first brother of Jesus. He was one of several brothers of Jesus mentioned in Matthew 13:55. Initially James did not believe in Jesus and questioned his purpose (John 7:2-5). Later he became a prominent leader in the early Christian church (Acts 15:13; see also 1 Corinthians 15:7; Galatians 2:9; Acts 12:17).

(3:1-6) Why would the teachers of the faith be held to greater accountability for what they say? What illustrations does James use to show how the tongue might be tamed? How does each illustration help to make his point? What does James say is the source of the evil done by the tongue?

(3:7-12) What is James suggesting that we are doing when we curse other human beings, who were made in the image of God? What illustrations are used here to contrast good and evil?

(3:13-16) What behavior shows evidence of wisdom from above? When is wisdom used for selfish ambition in today's world? How is this kind of wisdom of the devil?

(3:17-18) What are the qualities of wisdom from above? Contrast verse 18 with verse 16. Which of the characteristics of wisdom from above is most difficult for you? How will you try to develop it today?

What idea, verse, or phrase from this chapter can change your experience today?

Day 221
James 4

Background: Though his comments on works are often the primary point of discussion, the Letter of James is primarily a handbook of for living the faith. Section after section in chapters 3, 4, and 5 provide instructions for Christian living and behavior. These sections make us aware of the temptations of the devil and encourage us to resist them.

(4:1-3) In your own words, summarize the cause of conflict and disputes among Christians. What does this section teach you about prayer? Has there ever been a time when you have prayed with wrong motives? If so, when? What was the result of those prayers?

(4:4-6) What do you think is meant by "friendship with the world"? How does friendship with the world put one in opposition to God? In what ways are you tempted by the world and away from God?

(4:7-10) What 10 commands are given in these verses? Which of these speaks most clearly to you? How can humility lead God to exalt you?

(4:13-17) What words does James say we should use whenever we make plans? What does the use of these words demonstrate? What is suggested by not using these words?

What idea, verse, or phrase from this chapter can change your experience today?

Day 222
James 5

Background: James 5:1-6 appears to be the only section addressed to non-Christians. It may be, though, that James expected only his Christian readers would see this letter. This may have been his way of cautioning his readers against the love of money.

(5:1-6) For what actions does James condemn the wealthy? What will be their reward for this behavior? Who in today's world might fit these vivid descriptions? Has the pursuit of wealth ever gotten in the way of your relationship with God? If so, when?

(5:7-11) What is the "precious crop" for which we wait? What particular circumstances call for patience? What two examples are given for this kind of patience? What promise is given for those who persevere?

(5:12) How are James' words in this verse like those of Jesus in Matthew 5:33-37? With what expressions do people fail to heed this warning?

(5:13-16) In what specific circumstances does James encourage us to pray? Do you think James is wrong about prayers offered for healing? Explain.

(5:19-20) Who do you know who is wandering away from God's holy truth in Jesus Christ? What will you do today to turn this individual back to the Lord?

What idea, verse, or phrase from this chapter can change your experience today?

Day 223
1 Peter 1

Background: The author of this letter identifies himself as the disciple and apostle Peter. There is adequate material in this letter to support his claim: 1:12 refers to Peter's presence on the Day of Pentecost; 5:1-2 his attendance at the crucifixion of Christ; 5:5 may refer to the lesson he learned at the Last Supper as Jesus washed his feet; and in 5:13, he speaks of the close relationship he had with Mark, whose gospel may be based on the narratives of Peter.

(1:1-2) Which of the descriptions used by Peter in his greeting apply to you?

(1:3-9) What has God given us through the death and resurrection of Jesus Christ? What should be our attitude in light of these gifts from God? What purpose do suffering and trials serve? How are Peter's words in verse 8 like those of Jesus in John 20:29?

(1:13-16) What behavior does Peter expect of those who believe? What action do you think might be expected of the believer? What does it mean to be holy?

(1:17-21) What does Peter tell us about God? How does Peter show the contrast between the worldly and the heavenly? In what ways does Peter describe Jesus?

What idea, verse, or phrase from this chapter can change your experience today?

Day 224
1 Peter 2

Background: Much of this letter of Peter applies Christian doctrine to daily living. One of these applications has to do with our relationship to those in authority. Peter sees the role of authority as necessary for fulfilling the will of God. God places these people in positions of authority for the good of all.

(2:1-3) Of what behaviors does Peter tell us to rid ourselves? Why should we do this (see 1:22-23)? How does Peter illustrate the passion we should feel for growing in our relationship with God? What is God's "spiritual milk"? How is a longing for "spiritual milk" present in your life?

(2:4-8) In what ways is "living stone" a good description for Christ Jesus? How are you a living stone? What is the building of which Christ is making you a part? What does it mean to be part of a holy priesthood? What spiritual sacrifices are you making?

(2:9-10) How does Peter describe those who believe in Jesus? What is the mission of those whom God has called to faith? How has your faith in Jesus made you what you were not?

(2:13-17) How can doing good stop generalized accusations against Christians? How does showing respect for those in authority demonstrate a commitment to putting God first?

What idea, verse, or phrase from this chapter can change your experience today?

Day 225
1 Peter 3

Background: In this letter, Peter wants to encourage his readers to stand strong in the faith in the midst of persecution and suffering. This persecution was most severe under the rule of the Roman emperor, Domitian (81-96 A.D.), but began under the reign of Nero (54-68 A.D.). It was most likely during this earlier period of time that 1 Peter was written.

(3:1-6) How can submissive behavior on the part of a wife serve as a Christian witness to her husband? How can this teaching apply to other occasions for Christian witness? What does Peter say is true beauty for the Christian?

(3:7) What should motivate a husband's attitude toward his wife? Toward what purpose should this behavior be pursued?

(3:8-12) To what have we been called? For what reason? What virtues does Peter suggest will help us to remain strong in the faith? Which of these virtues is most difficult for you? How will you try to develop this virtue this week?

(3:15-16) What is the "defense to anyone who demands from you an accounting for the hope that is in you"? If this is difficult for you to explain, what will you do so that you will "always be ready"?

What idea, verse, or phrase from this chapter can change your experience today?

Day 226
1 Peter 4

Background: A key way that Peter encourages his readers to bear up through suffering is by the example of Jesus. Peter suggests that any suffering or persecution unites us further with Christ Jesus. The better we are able to adopt the attitude of Christ in the midst of his sufferings, the better we will be able to persevere.

(4:1-6) How do the trials of life make sinful desires less important to a person? What reason is given for the suffering experienced by the readers of this letter? Have you ever experienced this kind of abuse? If so, when? What two reasons are given for the proclaiming of the gospel?

(4:7-11)) What instructions does Peter give regarding the following:

the attitude for prayer:

the purpose of love:

the attitude for hospitality:

the use of gifts:

the manner of Christian speech:

the manner of Christian service:

(4:12-19) What attitude and behavior does Peter encourage for those who suffer as Christians? What will be the result of suffering because of one's faith?

What idea, verse, or phrase from this chapter can change your experience today?

Day 227
1 Peter 5

Background: Peter tells us in 5:13 that he is in Babylon at the time of this writing. Possible locations for this Babylon include a military outpost called Egyptian Babylon and a small city on the Euphrates River called Babylon. It also may have been a symbolic reference to the Babylonian exile of the Old Testament, though this seems less likely.

(5:1-4) With what attitude should elders or pastors serve their congregations? What behaviors should they practice? How is this instruction a fulfillment of Peter's last recorded conversation with Jesus in John 21:15-17?

(5:5-7) What instruction is given here for younger pastors or elders? Do you agree or disagree with this teaching? Explain. How might this instruction make for healthy leadership in a church? What has been your reaction to those who have led with a humble attitude? What instruction is given for church leaders in time of struggle?

(5:8-9) Might this be a lesson Peter learned during the night before Christ's death (see Matthew 26:36-46, 69-75)? Explain. What does Peter suggest about the relationship you have with other Christians?

(5:10-11) What promise is given for those who are steadfast in the faith?

What idea, verse, or phrase from this chapter can change your experience today?

Day 228
2 Peter 1

Background: 2 Peter contains some obvious similarities to the Letter of Jude, though there are differences, too. This type of borrowing and adapting another writing is common in ancient writings (as Matthew and Luke borrowed from Mark for their gospels). While some have suggested Jude used Peter's writing, it seems more likely that the longer second letter of Peter incorporated the shorter letter of Jude.

(1:1-2) How is this greeting similar to the greeting in Peter's first letter (1 Peter 1:1-2)? How are these two greetings different?

(1:3-4) What does Peter say that we have received through faith? For what purpose have we received these things?

(1:5-11) What attributes does Peter encourage us to adopt? How does each behavior lead to the next? Where are you in the development of these attributes? What benefit can these behaviors provide?

(1:12-15) How does Peter describe the human body? Why is this a good way to think about our earthly existence? What is Peter's goal before he dies? What do you want to impart before your life is over and to whom?

What idea, verse, or phrase from this chapter can change your experience today?

Day 229
2 Peter 2

Background: Peter's first letter sought to teach Christians how to deal with persecution and suffering that comes because of their faith. In this letter his goal is to instruct his readers on dealing with false teachers and evildoers who are active in the church. As in his first letter, Peter seeks to offer a balance of Christian doctrine and practical application.

(2:1-3) What will be the result of the words of false teachers in the church? What is their motivation? What is Jesus' relationship with the false teachers?

(2:4-10a) What three examples does Peter give to illustrate how God will save the godly and destroy the wicked? What are the two obvious sinful behaviors of these evil people (verse 10)?

(2:13-16) What behaviors and attitudes will reveal the ungodly teachers? Upon whom are they most likely to prey? What payment will they receive for their false teachings?

(2:17-22) How does Peter visually describe these false teachers? Who in the church are most likely to be swayed by these false teachings? Do you agree with Peter's words in verses 20 and 21? Why or why not? What does verse 22 suggest about the degree to which these false teachers had adopted the good news of Jesus Christ?

What idea, verse, or phrase from this chapter can change your experience today?

Day 230
2 Peter 3

Background: Peter closes this letter with some words of encouragement based on the second coming of Christ. As the end of his life draws near (2:13-14), Peter wants to give his readers some words of hope that will carry them through future days of suffering, persecution, disappointment, or whatever else they may face.

(3:1-2) What does Peter say is his primary purpose in writing this and his previous letters?

(3:3-7) What two examples does Peter cite to show the fallacy of the claim that the second coming will not take place? How do these examples make Peter's point? What does Peter say lies ahead for the wickedness of the world today?

(3:8-10) What does Peter teach here about God's understanding of time? What does he say about the nature of God? How does this explain the fact that the second coming has not yet happened? What warning does he give about the second coming of Christ?

(3:11-14) How are we to live until the Lord's return? Why can we look forward to that day with hope and joy instead of fear and despair? How are you striving to be found at peace with God? What will you do today to grow in that relationship?

What idea, verse, or phrase from this chapter can change your experience today?

Day 231
1 John 1

Background: Most scholars believe that the apostle John, the son of Zebedee and disciple of Jesus, wrote the three letters of John. Though John does not identify himself as the author of this first letter, many similarities between this letter and his gospel support his authorship. John is also the author of the two letters that follow this one and the Book of Revelation.

Compare the following passages from this First Letter of John and the Gospel of John. What similarities do you find?

1 John	Gospel of John	Similarities
1:1	1:1, 14	
1:4	6:24	
1:6-7	3:19-21	
2:7	13:34-35	
3:8	8:44	
3:14	5:24	
4:6	8:47	
4:9	1:14, 18; 3:16	
5:9	5:32, 37	
5:12	3:36	

(1:1-4) What is it that John proclaims here? What is John's goal in writing this? How will writing this make his joy complete? To whom would sharing the good news of Jesus give you joy?

(1:8-10) What happens when we deny our sins? What happens when we confess them? What sins do you need to confess today?

What idea, verse, or phrase from this chapter can change your experience today?

Day 232
1 John 2

Background: One of John's central purposes in writing this letter was to address the heresy of Gnosticism. Gnosticism taught that spirit is entirely good and matter is entirely evil. The Gnostics argued that Christ was spirit (good) and not human (evil). They argued that Christ only seemed to have a body, or that Christ (the spirit) entered Jesus (the man) at baptism and left him before death.

(2:1-2) What reason does John give for writing this letter? What is offered to those who sin? To whom is this available? What qualifies Jesus to speak for us?

(2:3-6) What behaviors characterize a believer? How do these behaviors reveal love for God? How are you seeking to "walk the walk" of Jesus?

(2:9-11) What does light and darkness represent in this discussion? What attitudes reveal the paths that a person is walking? Are there any ways in which you are walking in darkness? Explain. How will you try to walk in the light today?

(2:15-17) Against what worldly behaviors does John warn? Who does the world in this case represent? What worldly practices are prevalent today? How can these behaviors lead away from the love of God?

What idea, verse, or phrase from this chapter can change your experience today?

Day 233
1 John 3

Background: A key theme throughout this letter is that of Christian love. John wants his readers to understand that one way of measuring the truth of the message of others is by evaluating their commitment to Christian love. Furthermore, it is through our examples of Christian love that we show ourselves to truly be followers of Christ.

(3:1-3) How do we become part of God's family (see also John 1:12)? What does it mean to you that you are a child of God? How is this a good description of our relationship to God? What is the hope that belongs to the children of God?

(3:4-10) How does the love of God lead us to resist sinful living? What does John say about those who seek to continue to sin? How might Christians overcome the devil? What sinful behavior has been most difficult for you to give up? Ask God for strength.

(3:16-20) How was God's tremendous love for the world made known? What sacrifice are you willing to make in response to God's love? What is the most effective way we are to show this love in our lives? How will you show God's love today?

(3:21-24) What are the two parts of the command given us by God? Which part of this command is more difficult for you?

What idea, verse, or phrase from this chapter can change your experience today?

Day 234
1 John 4

Background: The letters of John are sometimes called "God's love letters." In this letter alone, John uses the word love in various forms a total of 43 times; in 4:7-5:3 it is used 32 times. For John, the sacrificial love of God is what draws us to God. Then, it is through our love for one another that others will see that love of God alive in us.

(4:1-3) What behavior shows a person to be moved by the Holy Spirit? What behavior shows a person to be moved by the spirit of the antichrist? What do these verses tell you about "antichrists"? 2:18-19, 22-23; 4:2; 2 John 7; 2 Thessalonians 2:3-4; Revelation 13:1-10

(4:4-6) Who is the "one who is in you"? Who is the "one who is in the world"? How can we distinguish between these two types of people? Name some of those who are most special to you who also have the one who is in you.

(4:7-12) What proof do we have of God's love? To what will the love of God move us? How can we see God who no one has ever seen?

(4:13-21) What is the relationship between love, fear, and punishment? Who acted first to establish our relationship with God? How does love for God but not for others make us liars? What is Jesus' ultimate command to us?

What idea, verse, or phrase from this chapter can change your experience today?

Day 235
1 John 5

Background: While John's gospel was written to bring people to faith, this letter was written to renew that faith as false teachers were threatening it. John wants to anchor his readers in the good news that Jesus, true God and true man, died to take away our sins. This act of love frees us to love others sacrificially, as God first loved us.

(5:1-5) What is the connection between faith and love? What is the relationship between love and God's commands? Are God's commands light or easy? Explain. How is it that we overcome the sinful behaviors of worldly living?

(5:6-12) What three things witness to us about the love of God? How do they agree with each other? What is the testimony that God has given to us?

(5:13) What does John say is his purpose for writing this letter?

(5:14-17) What important qualification does John give about our focus in praying? To what type of prayer does John encourage us to give special attention? What promise is given regarding this kind of prayer? For whom will you offer this special kind of prayer today?

(5:18-20) What three truths does John state in this closing to his first letter? How have you experienced each of these truths?

What idea, verse, or phrase from this chapter can change your experience today?

Day 236
2 John

Background: During the first century, missionary preachers carried the gospel message from town to town. Believers hosted these missionaries and took them into their homes. False teachers also followed this practice. The purpose of this letter is to assist readers in discerning between false missionaries and Christian missionaries.

(1-2) Who do you think might be "the elect lady and her children" to whom John the elder writes (consider verse 13 in your answer)? What is the "truth" which they all share (see John 14:6)?

(4-6) What is the command from God of which John reminds his readers? How does John define love? In what ways will you seek to keep this command today?

(7-9) How are those who do not acknowledge the incarnation of God (God becoming human in flesh) described? What danger stands before those who follow their teachings? How can one recognize these false teachers?

(10-11) On what basis should hospitality be extended? How would welcoming a false teacher cause one to share in the wicked work of that person? To whom could you offer Christian hospitality in today's world?

What idea, verse, or phrase from this chapter can change your experience today?

Day 237
3 John

Background: Apparently the leader of one church rejected some traveling teachers sent by John. This leader, Diotrephes, went so far as to excommunicate (expel) those members who had offered hospitality to John's messengers. John sends this letter to his Christian friend, Gaius, to praise him for supporting the teachers. At the same time, John criticizes Diotrephes and warns him of continuing such behavior.

(1) What important quality does John attribute to Gaius? Again, to what does this refer?

(2-4) For what does John commend Gaius? What might others report about you?

(5-8) What key things does John suggest with regard to showing Christian hospitality? To what purpose should this be done?

(9-10) For what behaviors is Diotrephes criticized? What seems to be his motivation in such behavior? What do you believe should be our motivation in the things we do?

(11-12) What behavior does John encourage? What is the source of such behavior? How does John intend to treat his opponent?

What idea, verse, or phrase from this chapter can change your experience today?

Day 238
Jude

Background: Many scholars believe that the author of this letter is Jude (another form of the common name Judas), the brother of Jesus (Matthew 13:55; Mark 6:3). He writes to warn his readers about certain false teachers who were perverting the message of God's grace. They claimed that since we are saved by grace, we can do whatever we wish since these sins would not be held against us.

(3-4) About what had Jude hoped to write? What caused Jude to change the focus of his letter? What is the message these false teachers offer? What tells you that their message is a lie?

(5-10) What three examples of divine judgment does Jude give? What three practices have these false teachers followed that will bring divine judgment upon themselves?

(17-19) What was the prediction of the apostles that has now come true? What danger to the believing community accompanies the message of these false teachers? What behavior of theirs will cause this to happen?

(20-23) What guidance is given for resisting these false teachers? How might active involvement in a Christian community help one resist false teachings? What responsibility do mature Christians have toward those who are newer to the faith? Who will you mentor in the faith during the next month?

What idea, verse, or phrase from this chapter can change your experience today?

Day 239
Revelation 1

Background: The author identifies himself as John. The early church believed this to be John the apostle, the disciple of Jesus. Others have suggested that the author was another John, whose name is mentioned in other ancient writings. While many today support the second theory, the overwhelming evidence supports the first opinion.

(1:1-3) What is the source of this revelation? How was it delivered? Why was it necessary for this revelation to be given? What promise is made to those who read or hear it?

(1:4-8) In what ways is Jesus described here? What greeting wish does Jesus offer? What is the significance of the description Jesus gives of himself using the first and last letters of the Greek alphabet (alpha and omega)?

(1:9-11) What information does John give about himself? What three things does John say we share in common? What specific information is given here that was first referred to in verse 4?

(1:12-20) What are the "seven lampstands"? What are the "seven stars"? How is Jesus (the Son of Man) described here? What is the symbolism of this description (see Exodus 28:3-4)? What is the significance of the "two-edged sword" (see Hebrews 4:12)?

(1:17-18) How does this description of Jesus relate to verse 8?

What idea, verse, or phrase from this chapter can change your experience today?

Day 240
Revelation 2

Background: Revelation is apocalyptic literature making great use of symbolism. Apocalyptic literature (like Daniel 10-12) speaks about the end times. It is usually written during times of great oppression and primarily seeks to encourage its readers to stand firm during trial.

(2:1-7) For what is the church in Ephesus commended? For what is this congregation criticized? What promise is made to those who remain faithful?

(2:8-11) For what is the church in Smyrna commended? For what is this congregation criticized? What promise is made to those who remain faithful?

(2:12-17) For what is the church in Pergamum commended? For what is this congregation criticized? What promise is made to those who remain faithful?

(2:18-29) For what is the church in Thyatira commended? For what is this congregation criticized? What promise is made to those who remain faithful?

How is your congregation like these churches? How is it different?

What idea, verse, or phrase from this chapter can change your experience today?

Day 241
Revelation 3

Background: The Book of Revelation is written in "code" because of the extreme persecution experienced by Christians in that time. Christians would understand many of the references while the pagans who persecuted them would not. Part of the challenge of reading Revelation is "decoding" its message of hope and encouragement.

(3:1-6) For what is the church in Sardis praised? For what is this congregation reprimanded? What promise is made to those who remain faithful?

(3:7-13) For what is the church in Philadelphia praised? For what is this congregation reprimanded? What promise is made to those who remain faithful?

(3:14-21) For what is the church in Laodicea praised? For what is this congregation reprimanded? What promise is made to those who remain faithful?

How is your congregation like these churches? How is it different?

(3:20) Do you understand this verse in an individual or corporate sense? What does the context of this section suggest about these words?

What idea, verse, or phrase from this chapter can change your experience today?

Day 242
Revelation 4

Background: Numerology (qualities attributed to numbers) is very important in this period of time and especially in this writing. The number seven is the most notable of all numbers mentioned in Revelation. In the Bible, seven represents perfection or completeness. Recall that the Ten Commandments (Exodus 20:1-17) are divided into two parts. The first three (the number of God) talk about our relationship to God. The last seven (the number for God–3–plus the number for the world–4) define how God wants us to relate to one another. When we follow all these, we are more complete.

What is your overall impression of heaven?

(4:1-6a) Who do you think sits on the throne? Why is this person described with colors? What is the significance of the lightening and thunder from the throne (see Exodus 19:16-19; Matthew 28:2-3; Acts 9:1-5)? What do the 24 thrones around the one suggest?

(4:6b-11) How does this vision of the four living creatures compare with Ezekiel's vision (Ezekiel 1:1-14)? Because they are covered with eyes, what do you think is one responsibility of the four living creatures? What does the response of the 24 elders to the giving of glory by the four creatures suggest?

(4:11) Why is God to be praised? Of what does God deserve to receive?

What idea, verse, or phrase from this chapter can change your experience today?

Day 243
Revelation 5

Background: The descriptions of animals and creatures in Revelation may seem rather grotesque at times. Much of this imagery, though, has symbolic meaning. Stars can refer to angels. A sash designates one who serves a priestly function. Eyes represent watchfulness and knowledge. Multiple heads stand for wisdom. A two-edged sword indicates judgment. Horns are symbolic of power or strength.

(5:1-5) What might the seven seals on the scroll suggest? What might this say about the one who holds the scroll? Who is the Lion of Judah (see Genesis 49:8-10; Matthew 1:1-3) and the Root of David (see Isaiah 11:1, 10; Matthew 1:1, 6)? What does this tell you about the one who has triumphed?

(5:4-6) The Lion of Judah is the triumphant conqueror expected by John and the Jewish people. The Lamb is the sacrifice made for the sins of the people. How does Jesus fulfill both these roles? What more are you told about Jesus here?

(5:7-14) How is the Lamb treated by the many beings of heaven? What do you notice about the frequency and style of honor and worship in heaven? What does this say to you about worship in our earthly life?

(5:9-10, 12, 13) What do these three hymns teach you about God and Jesus the Lamb? What does the Lamb deserve? How will you offer them today?

What idea, verse, or phrase from this chapter can change your experience today?

Day 244
Revelation 6

Background: Colors are also carry meaningful symbolism in Revelation. Purple is the color of royalty. Those who wear gold are noble and deserving of honor and praise. White can mean blessedness, purity, or holiness, or it can represent conquest. Red stands for blood, particularly in sacrifice, but can also mean bloodshed and war. Black can mean famine and judgment. Pale or ashen represents death.

The four horsemen, released from the first four seals (6:1-8), recall the imagery of Zechariah 1:8. What does each of these images represent?

(6:1-2)

(6:3-4)

(6:5-6)

(6:7-8)

(6:9-11) Why might those who died for their faith be placed under the protection of the altar? Of what importance is it that they are given white robes to wear?

(6:12-17) What do the earthquake and the blood red moon announce (see Acts 2:20)? What do the falling stars forewarn (see Mark 13:25-26)?

What idea, verse, or phrase from this chapter can change your experience today?

Day 245
Revelation 7

Background: Again, three is the number for God and four the number for the world (four seasons, a day is four six-hour sections, and so forth). When the world follows God's will, there is perfection (3+4=7). Twelve (3x4) also represents the world following God's will. In this chapter, the number 24 (12+12) stands for the twelve tribes of Israel (people from the Old Testament) and the twelve disciples of Jesus (people from the New Testament). Numbers multiplied by 1,000 (such as 12,000) are not necessarily literal, but more likely mean a great quantity.

(7:1-8) Who do the 144,000 represent? When did you receive God's seal on your forehead? The mark given to the seal on Hebrew scrolls was the last letter of the Hebrew alphabet, Taw, made like an X or a +. With what sign were you sealed? What is the significance of this sign?

(7:9-10) Who is included in this great multitude? Why might they be dressed in white robes? Why might they be carrying palm branches (see Leviticus 23:40; John 12:13)?

(7:12) What attributes are offered to God in this hymn? How does that compare with previous hymns (4:11; 5:12, 13)?

(7:13-17) What is meant by washing and made white in the blood of the Lamb? What promise is made to these persecuted faithful? What part of this promise is most appealing to you?

What idea, verse, or phrase from this chapter can change your experience today?

Day 246
Revelation 8

Background: John was the last of the disciples to die and probably the only one still alive at the time this book was written. John understood the persecution under which his readers suffered and against which he encouraged them to stand firm. He had and recorded this vision while on the island of Patmos, probably the site of a Roman penal colony. Patmos is a small, rocky island about four miles by eight miles off the coast of Ephesus in the Aegean Sea.

(8:3-5) What does the censer first bring before God? What does the censer then bring upon the rest of the earth?

The trumpet serves to announce important events or to give commands in time of war. What does each of these trumpets announce?

(8:7)

(8:8-9)

(8:10-11)

(8:12)

(8:1-12) What portion of creation is affected by these events? Who is the source of this judgment (see verse 2)? Upon whom does this judgment fall (note the order of events in verses 3-5)?

What idea, verse, or phrase from this chapter can change your experience today?

Day 247
Revelation 9

Background: The abyss is the subterranean or underground place where hoards of demons dwell. It has the connotation of being very deep or even bottomless. When Jesus healed the man possessed by a legion of demons, they begged him not to send them into the abyss (Luke 8:26-33). Seven of the nine New Testament occurrences of this word are in the Book of Revelation.

(9:1-6) What did the fifth seal release upon the earth and what power is given to them? For how long will they have power? Whom do these creatures afflict? Who is protected from them? What will be the result of their torture?

(9:7-12) The faces of these creatures are human, suggesting intelligence and cunning. What do the other features suggest?

(9:13-19) What does verse 15 suggest about God? What portion of humanity is affected by the events of this trumpet? What part of humanity is it that is affected (see verse 4)? What does verse 19 suggest about the origin of these horses and their riders?

(9:20-21) What does this suggest was the purpose of the preceding events? What behaviors led to this judgment and punishment upon the earth? Do you see this kind of behavior in the world today? If so, where?

What idea, verse, or phrase from this chapter can change your experience today?

Day 248
Revelation 10

Background: In apocalyptic writings, mysteries are secrets, kept in heaven but revealed to the apocalyptic writers. This revelation to John is that the whole purpose of God in human history is coming to a close according to God's own timeline. When it has finished playing out, God's purpose will be fully realized, evil will be overthrown completely, questions will be answered, and wrongs will be righted.

(10:1-4) What does the rainbow over the head of the angel recall (see Genesis 9:8-17)? Of what are the legs like pillars of fire reminiscent (see Exodus 13:21-22; 14:19, 24)? What might these to symbols suggest to those who put their trust in God?

(10:5-7) What might it suggest that this angel stands on both land and sea? What qualities of God are mentioned here? How would this be of comfort to those under persecution? What was the cause of the delay mentioned in verse 6 (see 6:9-11)?

(10:8-10) How do you seek to eat—to fully take in and digest the message of God for your life? What part of the message of this revelation is sweet to you? What part of this message is bitter?

(10:11) What responsibility comes to those to whom the word of God is revealed? How are you seeking to do this regularly in your daily life?

What idea, verse, or phrase from this chapter can change your experience today?

Day 249
Revelation 11

Background: 1,260 days is equal to 42 thirty-day months. 42 months is three-and-a-half years (or "a time, and times, and half a time" in Revelation 12:14). (This three-and-a-half-year period may come from the dividing in half of the seventieth "seven" from Daniel 9:24-27.) This period of time became symbolic for a limited period of unrestrained wickedness and suffering.

(11:1-6) What clues from this section help in identifying the two witnesses (olive trees and lampstands) of God (see 1 Kings 17:1; 2 Kings 1:10, 12; Exodus 7:17-21)? To whom do they show obedience? What meaning would these two figures have for believers (see Matthew 17:1-3)?

(11:7-10) What does the origin of the beast say about it? What do Sodom and Egypt suggest about those who will view their bodies (see Genesis 18:20-21, 19:24-25; Exodus 1:8-14)? What does the three-and-a-half days suggest in comparison to the three-and-a-half years of verse 3?

(11:11-12) What will God do for the two faithful witnesses killed by the beast? What promise does this act hold for those who are faithful?

(11:15-19) How does verse 17 differ from 1:4, 8 and 4:8? What does this say about God?

What idea, verse, or phrase from this chapter can change your experience today?

Day 250
Revelation 12

Background: Another characteristic of apocalyptic literature is that of dualism—two things that stand in contrast to or battle with each other. In the Book of Revelation, examples of this contrast are the present world and the perfect future world and the present age under Satan's rule and the future age under God's direction. Examples of dualistic battles include those between God and Satan, good and evil, and angels and demons.

(12:1-6) The woman in this image probably represents that faithful community which looks to the coming of the Messiah. Who might the twelve stars represent? Who is the son to whom she gives birth? What does the iron scepter suggest?

(12:7-9) Look at Daniel 12:1. What does this tell you about Michael? Who is the dragon?

(12:10-12) How is the dragon, Satan, described in this passage (see also Zechariah 3:1)? How was Satan overcome? What does this victory mean for the faithful? What awaits those who have chosen the ways of the world?

(12:13-17) What act enraged the dragon that is Satan? What does it mean that he pursued the woman who gave birth to the child? How did God intervene on her behalf? How did the dragon respond? Interpret this in terms of worldly events.

What idea, verse, or phrase from this chapter can change your experience today?

Day 251
Revelation 13

Background: Even as there is a Holy Trinity—Father, Son, and Holy Spirit—Revelation includes an unholy trinity. The dragon is Satan, or the devil (12:9). The beast out of the sea (13:1) represents the antichrist and suggests secular authority that opposes Christianity (such as the emperors of Rome). The beast out of the earth is the false prophet of 16:13; 19:20, and 20:10, and is the personification of those religious powers that choose to serve the worldly authorities.

(13:1-4) How does the beast out of the sea compare with the one in Daniel 17:2-7? What is the relationship between the dragon and this beast? What does the completely healed fatal wound on the beast suggest about its power? How does the world react to this?

(13:5-10) What is the work of the beast from the sea? Who are those that display this kind of behavior in today's world? Against whom are those who worship the beast contrasted? What instruction or encouragement is given to the faithful in Christ?

(13:11-14) As what does this beast from the earth try to appear? What reveals its true identity? How does this fit with Jesus' warning in Matthew 7:15?

(13:15-18) What is the work of the beast out of the earth? How does this second beast relate to the first beast? How do religious leaders or groups fall under the authority of secular leaders and powers?

What idea, verse, or phrase from this chapter can change your experience today?

Day 252
Revelation 14

Background: The number 666 in 13:18 has been a key point of speculation for centuries. It is probably best understood as representing the trinity of evil and imperfection. Just as a musical instrument sounds more inharmonious as it gets closer to being in tune, the number 6 is more imperfect because of its nearness to the number 7.

(14:1-5) Where are the 144,000 in this passage? What emotion do they and heaven seem to display? What qualities and behaviors characterize them? What are these faithful people able to do?

(14:6-7) What gospel message would you announce? Try to proclaim it to someone this week.

(14:8) How does this passage suggest this prostitute seduced her victims? What does this imply about the political and religious powers who follow worldly ways?

(14:9-13) What awaits those who turn away from God? What helps you to wait patiently and remain faithful for the day of the Lord?

(14:14-20) Who is the one "like the Son of Man" (see Matthew 12:40; 19:28; John 3:14; Acts 7:56)? What is being portrayed in this passage?

What idea, verse, or phrase from this chapter can change your experience today?

Day 253
Revelation 15

Background: The Romans believed in many gods and often worshiped the emperor as a god. Christianity, which teaches belief in the one God, threatened this emperor worship. This was one of the main reasons for the persecution of the Christians. The judgment of Revelation upon the earth was a promise to those early Christians that those who caused them to suffer would one day receive divine judgment.

(15:1) What characteristic of God is emphasized in this passage? Why would John call this a marvelous sign? Do you think much about this aspect of God? Why or why not?

(15:2) Who stands beside the sea in this image? Over what three individuals or groups have they been victorious? What might this suggest to the readers of this book in John's day? What does this suggest to you today?

(15:3-4) Compare the song of the Lamb here with the song of Moses in Exodus 15:18. How are they the same? How are they different? Who is the central focus of each of these hymns?

(15:5-8) What seems about to happen? What does it mean that now no one can enter the temple until the seven plagues are completed?

What idea, verse, or phrase from this chapter can change your experience today?

Day 254
Revelation 16

Background: Throughout Revelation, God's judgment upon the wicked and unfaithful comes as plagues and visions of great destruction. Many of these recall the judgment and punishment visited upon Egypt for Pharaoh's failure to release the Israelites from their slavery. Compare 8:7 with Exodus 9:13-25; 8:8 with Exodus 7:20-21; and 8:12 with Exodus 10:21-23. Be mindful of this as you read of the plagues in this chapter.

(16:1-12) Compare each of these plagues with the one from Exodus and list that part of creation affected by each plague:

Revelation 16:2 and Exodus 9:9-11:

Revelation 16:3 and Exodus 7:17-18:

Revelation 16:4 and Exodus 7:20-21:

Revelation 16:10-11 and Exodus 10:21-22:

(16:13-14) Whom do these foul spirits like frogs serve? What is the job of these demonic spirits?

(16:15) Who is speaking in this verse (see Matthew 24:42-44)? How are you keeping watch?

(16:17-21) What is the result of this last bowl? What portion of the earth does it seem to affect? How do the unfaithful react to God's wrath upon the earth?

What idea, verse, or phrase from this chapter can change your experience today?

Day 255
Revelation 17

Background: Ancient Babylon, in the area of modern Iraq, was the political, commercial, and religious center of an Old Testament empire. It was well known for the immoral behavior of its citizens. While it surely represented Rome in John's day, it suggests for us any worldly political or religious system that seeks to follow worldly values and opposes God and God's faithful.

(17:1-2) Who is the great whore (see 14:8)? How have earthly rulers behaved in relation to this woman? How have those with worldly values responded to the kings and the woman? When have you seen this response in the world today?

(17:3-6) Which beast is portrayed here (compare 13:1 with 13:11)? What names or titles do people give themselves today that suggest that they are equal to or greater than God? What does verse 6 suggest has been the work of the woman?

(17:7-8) How is the description of the beast in verse 8 like the one of Jesus in 1:4? How do these descriptions differ? What does this suggest about the beast? What warning about the beast is given in this description? What promise or hope is given to us in reference to the beast? Why might this astonish those who chose to follow the beast?

(17:14) What encouragement does this verse give? How can you show this hope in your life?

What idea, verse, or phrase from this chapter can change your experience today?

Day 256
Revelation 18

Background: The lament for Babylon presented in this chapter (18:9-20) echoes Ezekiel's lament for Tyre in Ezekiel 27. In fact, the similarity is so close that 15 of the 29 goods listed here are also listed in Ezekiel 27:12-22.

(18:1-3) How is Babylon the great now described? What effect did she have on the nations, the kings, and the merchants who followed her?

(18:4-8) In what ways does the voice from heaven call for the people to repent? In what ways have you looked toward Babylon and looked for which you need to repent? What does it suggest that God's punishment on Babylon will happen in one day?

(18:9-10) Why might the kings of the earth lament over Babylon's destruction?

(18:11-17a) Why do the merchants lament Babylon's defeat? Which of their goods reveal their true nature? Has this ruin happened quickly or taken a long time?

(18:20-24) Why do God's people rejoice over the destruction of Babylon? On what basis did God judge Babylon? What lesson is there in this judgment for you?

What idea, verse, or phrase from this chapter can change your experience today?

Day 257
Revelation 19

Background: The word Hallelujah occurs four times in this chapter and nowhere else in the New Testament. It is derived from two Hebrew words that mean "Praise the Lord." This section in Revelation follows the pattern of many of the "Praise" or "Hallel" psalms, particularly Psalm 135 and those following, that recall the saving acts of God.

(19:1-8) Who sings these words of praise to God? For what reasons is God praised? What does the image of a marriage suggest about the relationship between the Lamb of God and the Lamb's bride? Who does verse 8 suggest is the bride of the Lamb?

(19:9-10) How did God invite you to the marriage supper of the Lamb? How has this been a blessing? What lesson does the angel teach about worship? Who today fails to follow this lesson?

(19:11-16) How is the rider on this white horse different from the one in 6:2? Who is this rider? What qualities and characteristics are attributed to this rider? Have you ever thought of the rider in this way? Explain.

(19:17-18) How does the great supper of God contrast with the marriage feast of the Lamb? At which meal do you wish to eat? Why?

(19:19-21) What punishment awaits those who oppose the rider and his army?

What idea, verse, or phrase from this chapter can change your experience today?

Day 258
Revelation 20

Background: The image of punishment by fire is common in both Jewish and non-Jewish literature (see Matthew 5:22). John's description here fits very well with "Gehenna," a site of cultic sacrifice of human beings (see 2 Kings 16:3; 23:10; Jeremiah 7:31). This image came to be equated with the place of final punishment—hell.

(20:1-3) Why is Satan called the "ancient serpent" (see Genesis 3:1-5)? In comparison to 12:6; 13:5; 18:8, and 18:17, how long will Satan be bound? Then for how long will he be free?

(20:4-6) What awaits those who were martyred for their faith in Christ Jesus? In what ways did they show their faith? How are you showing your faith?

(20:7-10) What behavior demonstrates that Satan never changes, even after his confinement? What information suggests the size and scope of Satan's army? What will be the result of Satan's final attempt to defeat God?

(20:11-15) Who is seated on the throne? What suggests the extent of this being's authority? Who are those who now are resurrected for judgment? Who will come through God's judgment? What awaits those who do not pass this judgment?

What idea, verse, or phrase from this chapter can change your experience today?

Day 259
Revelation 21

Background: A new order and existence will come into being once Satan and his armies are defeated. The final two chapters of this book are a description of this new heaven and earth, and of the city that is the center of this new order—the New Jerusalem. This city combines elements of the old Jerusalem, the temple, and the Garden of Eden.

(21:1-4) What has happened to God's original creation as we know it? What is Christ's relationship to this new city (see also verse 10)? How are things different in this New Jerusalem?

(21:5-8) Who is seated on the throne (see 1:8)? What will be the relationship between him and the faithful? What does he promise to them? Who will not receive these blessings?

(21:9-14) What do these features in this description of the New Jerusalem tell you about the city?

"radiance like a very rare jewel, like jasper clear as crystal":

"twelve gates with the names of the tribes of Israel":

"twelve foundations with the names of the apostles":

(21:22-27) What is the significance of verse 22 (see 1 Kings 6:13)? How will this new city affect the world? What do the gates being open day and night suggest?

What idea, verse, or phrase from this chapter can change your experience today?

Day 260
Revelation 22

Background: The last two of seven beatitudes are included in this chapter, keeping to the pattern of completeness through the number seven. "Blessed" describes the favorable circumstances that come to us from God. Being blessed refers to the sense of spiritual ecstasy and contentment that comes only from God.

(22:1-5) What will life be like in the New Jerusalem with God? What does the tree of life suggest (see Genesis 2:9; 3:22)? What might it mean that this tree bears fruit for each month of the year? What will it mean for you to be in the presence of God?

Who are those blessed in each of these beatitudes?

1:3

14:13

16:15

19:9

20:6

20:7

20:14

(22:8-9) What lesson must John again be taught here? In what way are the faithful like the angels?

(22:12-16) What blessing does Jesus promise to the faithful? What warning does Jesus give to the readers of this book? How will you heed Jesus' warning and receive his promise?

What idea, verse, or phrase from this chapter can change your experience today?

Assigned Reading	Date Read	Assigned Reading	Date Read
Matthew 1		Matthew 26	
Matthew 2		Matthew 27	
Matthew 3		Matthew 28	
Matthew 4		Mark 1	
Matthew 5		Mark 2	
Matthew 6		Mark 3	
Matthew 7		Mark 4	
Matthew 8		Mark 5	
Matthew 9		Mark 6	
Matthew 10		Mark 7	
Matthew 11		Mark 8	
Matthew 12		Mark 9	
Matthew 13		Mark 10	
Matthew 14		Mark 11	
Matthew 15		Mark 12	
Matthew 16		Mark 13	
Matthew 17		Mark 14	
Matthew 18		Mark 15	
Matthew 19		Mark 16	
Matthew 20		Luke 1	
Matthew 21		Luke 2	
Matthew 22		Luke 3	
Matthew 23		Luke 4	
Matthew 24		Luke 5	
Matthew 25		Luke 6	

Assigned Reading	Date Read	Assigned Reading	Date Read
Luke 7		John 8	
Luke 8		John 9	
Luke 9		John 10	
Luke 10		John 11	
Luke 11		John 12	
Luke 12		John 13	
Luke 13		John 14	
Luke 14		John 15	
Luke 15		John 16	
Luke 16		John 17	
Luke 17		John 18	
Luke 18		John 19	
Luke 19		John 20	
Luke 20		John 21	
Luke 21		Acts 1	
Luke 22		Acts 2	
Luke 23		Acts 3	
Luke 24		Acts 4	
John 1		Acts 5	
John 2		Acts 6	
John 3		Acts 7	
John 4		Acts 8	
John 5		Acts 9	
John 6		Acts 10	
John 7		Acts 11	

Assigned Reading	Date Read	Assigned Reading	Date Read
Acts 12		Romans 9	
Acts 13		Romans 10	
Acts 14		Romans 11	
Acts 15		Romans 12	
Acts 16		Romans 13	
Acts 17		Romans 14	
Acts 18		Romans 15	
Acts 19		Romans 16	
Acts 20		1 Corinthians 1	
Acts 20		1 Corinthians 2	
Acts 22		1 Corinthians 3	
Acts 23		1 Corinthians 4	
Acts 24		1 Corinthians 5	
Acts 25		1 Corinthians 6	
Acts 26		1 Corinthians 7	
Acts 27		1 Corinthians 8	
Acts 28		1 Corinthians 9	
Romans 1		1 Corinthians 10	
Romans 2		1 Corinthians 11	
Romans 3		1 Corinthians 12	
Romans 4		1 Corinthians 13	
Romans 5		1 Corinthians 14	
Romans 6		1 Corinthians 15	
Romans 7		1 Corinthians 16	
Romans 8		2 Corinthians 1	

Assigned Reading	Date Read	Assigned Reading	Date Read
2 Corinthians 2		Philippians 2	
2 Corinthians 3		Philippians 3	
2 Corinthians 4		Philippians 4	
2 Corinthians 5		Colossians 1	
2 Corinthians 6		Colossians 2	
2 Corinthians 7		Colossians 3	
2 Corinthians 8		Colossians 4	
2 Corinthians 9		1 Thessalonians 1	
2 Corinthians 10		1 Thessalonians 2	
2 Corinthians 11		1 Thessalonians 3	
2 Corinthians 12		1 Thessalonians 4	
2 Corinthians 13		1 Thessalonians 5	
Galatians 1		2 Thessalonians 1	
Galatians 2		2 Thessalonians 2	
Galatians 3		2 Thessalonians 3	
Galatians 4		1 Timothy 1	
Galatians 5		1 Timothy 2	
Galatians 6		1 Timothy 3	
Ephesians 1		1 Timothy 4	
Ephesians 2		1 Timothy 5	
Ephesians 3		1 Timothy 6	
Ephesians 4		2 Timothy 1	
Ephesians 5		2 Timothy 2	
Ephesians 6		2 Timothy 3	
Philippians 1		2 Timothy 4	

Assigned Reading	Date Read	Assigned Reading	Date Read
Titus 1		1 Peter 4	
Titus 2		1 Peter 5	
Titus 3		2 Peter 1	
Philemon		2 Peter 2	
Hebrews 1		2 Peter 3	
Hebrews 2		1 John 1	
Hebrews 3		1 John 2	
Hebrews 4		1 John 3	
Hebrews 5		1 John 4	
Hebrews 6		1 John 5	
Hebrews 7		2 John	
Hebrews 8		3 John	
Hebrews 9		Jude	
Hebrews 10		Revelation 1	
Hebrews 11		Revelation 2	
Hebrews 12		Revelation 3	
Hebrews 13		Revelation 4	
James 1		Revelation 5	
James 2		Revelation 6	
James 3		Revelation 7	
James 4		Revelation 8	
James 5		Revelation 9	
1 Peter 1		Revelation 10	
1 Peter 2		Revelation 11	
1 Peter 3		Revelation 12	

Assigned Reading	Date Read	Assigned Reading	Date Read
Revelation 13		Revelation 18	
Revelation 14		Revelation 19	
Revelation 15		Revelation 20	
Revelation 16		Revelation 21	
Revelation 17		Revelation 22	

Notes